INTRODUCTION
To The Doublebit Press Legacy Edition

The old experts of the woods, mountains, and farm country life taught timeless principles and skills for decades. Through their books, the old experts offered rich descriptions of the outdoor world and encouraged learning through personal experiences in nature. Over the last 125 years, handcrafts, artisanal works, outdoors activities, and our experiences with nature have substantially changed. Many things have gotten simpler as equipment and processes have improved, and life outside, on the farm, or on the trail now brings with it many of the same comforts enjoyed in town. In addition, some activities of the old days are now no longer in vogue, or are even outright considered inappropriate or illegal. However, despite many of the positive changes in handcrafting, traditional skills, and outdoors methods that have occurred over the years, *there are many other skills and much knowledge that are at risk of being lost* that should never be forgotten.

By publishing Legacy Editions of classic texts on handcrafts, artisanal skills, nature lore, survival, and outdoors and camping life, it is our goal at Doublebit Press to do what we can to preserve and share the works from forgotten teachers that form the cornerstone of the authentic and hard-wrought American tradition of self-sustainability and self-reliance. Through remastered reprint editions of timeless classics of traditional crafts, classic methods, and outdoor recreation, perhaps we can regain some of this lost knowledge for future generations.

On the frontier, folks made virtually everything by hand. Old farmers' knowledge and homestead skills were passed on to the future generation because it meant survival. In addition, much of traditional handcrafts and outdoors life knowledge was passed on from American Indians – the original handcrafters and outdoorsmen of the Americas.

Today, much of the handcrafted items of the frontier are made in factories, only briefly seeing a human during the process (if at all). Making things by hand indeed takes much (often strenuous) work, but it provides an extreme sense of pride in the finished job. Instantly, all hand-made items come with a story on their creation. Most importantly, though, making items with traditional methods gives you experience and knowledge of how things work.

This is similar to the case of camping and the modern outdoors experience, with neatly arranged campsites at public campgrounds and camping gear that has been meticulously improved and tested in both the lab and the field. These changes have also caused us to lose this traditional knowledge, having it buried in the latest high-tech iteration of your latest camp gadget.

Many modern conveniences are only a brief trek away, with many parks, campgrounds, and even forests having easy-access roads, convenience stores, and even cell phone signal. In some ways, it is much easier to camp and go outdoors today, and that is a good thing! We should not be miserable when we go

THE FINE ART OF FISHING

A CLASSIC HANDBOOK ON SHORE, STREAM, CANOE, AND FLY FISHING EQUIPMENT AND TECHNIQUE FOR TROUT, BASS, SALMON, AND OTHER SPECIES

BY **SAMUEL G. CAMP**
ORIGINALLY PUBLISHED IN 1911

LEGACY EDITION

THE CLASSIC OUTING HANDBOOKS COLLECTION

BOOK 8

FEATURING

REMASTERED CLASSIC WORKS OF THE HIGHEST QUALITY FROM **THE TIMELESS MASTERS AND TEACHERS** OF TRADITIONAL HANDCRAFTS AND OUTDOORS SKILLS

Doublebit Press

New content, introduction, cover design, and annotations Copyright © 2020 by Doublebit Press. All rights reserved.

Doublebit Press is an imprint of Eagle Nest Press
www.doublebitpress.com | Cherry, IL, USA

Original content under the public domain. First published in 1911 by Samuel G. Camp.

This title, along with other Doublebit Press books are available at a volume discount for youth groups, outdoors clubs, craft groups, or reading groups. Contact us at info@doublebitpress.com for more information.

Doublebit Press Legacy Edition ISBNs
Hardcover: 978-1-64389-152-1
Paperback: 978-1-64389-153-8

Disclaimer: Because of its age and historic context, this text could contain content on present-day inappropriate outdoors activities, outdated medical information, unsafe chemical and mechanical processes, or culturally and racially insensitive content. Doublebit Press, or its employees, authors, and other affiliates, assume no liability for any actions performed by readers or any damages that might be related to information contained in this book. This text has been published for historical study and for personal literary enrichment toward the goal of the preservation of American outdoors and handcraft history and heritage.

First Doublebit Press Legacy Edition Printing, 2020

outside — lovers of the outdoors know the essential restorative capability that the woods can have on the body, mind, and soul. But to experience it, you need to not be surrounded by modern high-tech robotic coffee pots, tents that build themselves, or watches that tell you how to do everything!

Although things have gotten easier on us in the 21st Century when it comes to handcrafts and the outdoors, it certainly does not mean that we should forget the foundations of technical skills, artisanal production, and outdoors lore. All of the modern tools and cool gizmos that make our lives easier are all founded on principles of traditional methods that the old masters knew well and taught to those who would listen. We just have to look deeply into the design of our modern gadgets and factories to see the original methods and traditional skills at play.

Every woods master and artisan had their own curriculum or thought some things were more important than others. The old masters also taught common things in slightly different ways or did things differently than others. That's what makes each of the experts different and worth reading. There's no universal way of doing something, especially today. Learning to go about something differently helps with mastery or learn a new skill altogether. Basically, you learn intimately how things work, giving you great skill with adapting and being flexible when the need arises.

Again, to use the metaphor from the above paragraphs, traditional skills mastery consists of learning the basic building blocks of how and why the old artisans made things, how they lived outdoors, and why woods and nature lore mattered. Everything is intertwined, and doing it by hand increases your knowledge of this complex network. Each master goes about describing these building blocks differently or shows a different aspect of them.

Therefore, we have decided to publish this Legacy Edition reprint in our collection of traditional handcraft and outdoors life classics. This book is an important contribution to the early American traditional skills and outdoors literature, and has important historical and collector value toward preserving the American tradition of self-sufficiency and artisan production. The knowledge it holds is an invaluable reference for practicing outdoors skills and hand craft methods. Its chapters thoroughly discuss some of the essential building blocks of knowledge that are fundamental but may have been forgotten as equipment gets fancier and technology gets smarter. In short, this book was chosen for Legacy Edition printing because much of the basic skills and knowledge it contains has been forgotten or put to the wayside in trade for more modern conveniences and methods.

Although the editors at Doublebit Press are thrilled to have comfortable experiences in the woods and love our modern equipment for making cool hand-made projects, we are also realizing that the basic skills taught by the old masters are more essential than ever as our culture becomes more and more hooked on digital stuff. We don't want to risk forgetting the important steps, skills, or building blocks involved with each step of traditional methods. Sometimes, *there's no substitute for just doing something on your own, by hand.* Sometimes, to truly learn something is to *just do it by hand.* The Legacy Edition series represents the essential contributions to the American handcraft and outdoors tradition by the great experts.

With technology playing a major role in everyday life, sometimes we need to take a step back in time to find those basic building blocks used for gaining mastery – the things that we have luckily not completely lost and has been recorded in books over the last two centuries. These skills aren't forgotten, they've just been shelved. *It's time to unshelve them once again and reclaim the lost knowledge of self-sufficiency.*

Based on this commitment to preserving our outdoors and handcraft heritage, we have taken great pride in publishing this book as a complete original work without any editorial changes or revisions. We hope it is worthy of both study and collection by handcrafters and outdoors folk in the modern era and to fulfill its status as a Legacy Edition by passing along to the libraries of future generations.

Unlike many other low-resolution photocopy reproductions of classic books that are common on the market, this Legacy Edition does not simply place poor photography of old texts on our pages and use error-prone optical scanning or computer-generated text. We want our work to speak for itself and reflect the quality demanded by our customers who spend their hard-earned money. With this in mind, each Legacy Edition book that has been chosen for publication is carefully remastered from original print books, *with the Doublebit Legacy Edition printed and laid out in the exact way that it was presented at its original publication.* Our Legacy Edition books are inspired by the original covers of first-edition texts, embracing the beauty that is in both the simplicity and sometimes ornate decoration of vintage and antique books. We want provide a beautiful, memorable experience that is as true to the original text as best as possible, but with the aid of modern technology to make as meaningful a reading experience as possible for books that are typically over a century old.

Because of its age and because it is presented in its original form, the book may contain misspellings, inking errors, and other print blemishes that were common for the age. However, these are exactly the things that we feel give the book its character, which we preserved in this Legacy Edition. During digitization, we did our best to ensure that each illustration in the text was clean and sharp with the least amount of loss from being copied and digitized as possible. Full-page plate illustrations are presented as they were found, often including the extra blank page that was often behind a plate and plate pagination. For the covers, we use the original cover design as our template to give the book its original feel. We are sure you'll appreciate the fine touches and attention to detail that your Legacy Edition has to offer.

For traditional handcrafters and outdoors enthusiasts who demand the best from their equipment, this Doublebit Press Legacy Edition reprint was made with you in mind. Both important and minor details have equally both been accounted for by our publishing staff, down to the cover, font, layout, and images. It is the goal of Doublebit Legacy Edition series to preserve America's handcrafting and outdoors heritage, but also be cherished as collectible pieces, worthy of collection in any person's library and that can be passed to future generations.

Every book selected to be in this series offers unique views and instruction on important skills, advice, tips, tidbits, anecdotes, stories, and experiences that will enrich the repertoire of any person looking to learn the skills it contains. To learn the most basic building blocks leads to mastery of all its aspects.

Studying This Book

The pages within this book present an overwhelming amount of information, facts, and directions to memorize that are often outdated and at the least, out of practice by modern standards. That doesn't mean that these pages have nothing to teach! It's just going to likely be new stuff for many readers.

Our one suggestion is *don't try to memorize everything*, especially when you're thumbing through the book or even reading it cover-to-cover. Many of our Legacy Edition books are antique or vintage. These writings from the late 1800's to early 1900's can be dense and out of style for someone not used to reading these types of books. Instead, gain some basic familiarity with each topic by thumbing through the pages, looking at the illustrations, and seeing the section headers. Then, choose a few topics or skills for deeper study.

Before you start a crafting project, or before camping or other outdoors trips can even begin, some planning and reflection is useful. First, it might be helpful to read through the book with plans in mind. The book can provide useful material for close study and reflection before you acquire equipment or head out to the field to practice.

Secondly, once you've come up with a practice plan, you will of course want to start doing tasks and skills. Doublebit Legacy Edition reprints all represent *learning by doing*, with each book containing many skills to master that have long sense been out of practice. But this is exactly why we print these books – these skills and methods should not be forgotten!

Any of the old artisans and tutors of woodcraft will tell you in their classic books that you can only truly learn how do stuff by *actually doing it*. Home study indeed does you well by using the many guidebooks that have been published over the previous 125 years. However, hundreds more lessons will become immediately available to you the moment you start with some of the old-style tasks.

For instance, before the days of camping outfitters, outdoors adventurers made their gear, which was tailored to their individual needs. Many experiments were done in the field to tweak their gear to get that ever-changing point of "perfect." Aside from experiencing wonderful lessons in history, getting outside and doing some of the activities this book will give you an appreciation for modern advances in outdoors and handcraft method and tools of the trade, as well as a deeper understanding of the foundations of outdoors and hand-craft life in the event that your gear fails you or you otherwise find yourself in situations where knowing the principles will get you unstuck fast.

If we were to tally up each of the individual tips in the Doublebit Library of Legacy Edition reprints, they would easily number in the thousands. The old masters represent centuries of previous knowledge that have been all but lost to 21st Century, technology-driven folks. To this point, although experience and *actually doing stuff* are the best forms of learning, taking a mindful approach to study of these works also benefit your development as a competent outdoorsperson and handcrafter.

You may also find it invaluable to take these volumes with you on your camping or other outdoors trips. In addition to having reading material on a variety of topics in the field for down time, you'll also find a thousand things to try in these pages if you're bored. Although skills may be best studied when in the field through experience and reflection, you may also study woods skills at home as well. Gaining familiarity through reading, videos, and other media are a great start toward building your ability toward gaining mastery in the field.

THE FINE ART OF FISHING

BY

SAMUEL G. CAMP

Author of

"FISHING KITS & EQUIPMENT"

"The angler considers his sport as a fine art, of which merely to obtain fish is but a small part.... It is the way the thing is done."

H. P. Wells in "Fly-Rods & Fly-Tackle."

NEW YORK
OUTING PUBLISHING COMPANY
MCMXV

COPYRIGHT, 1911, BY
OUTING PUBLISHING COMPANY

FOREWORD

THE present volume is intended to supplement with notes on our common game fish and the practical use of the fly- and bait-casting rod in casting and in fishing the description of fly- and bait-casting tackle contained in the writer's previous book, "Fishing Kits and Equipment"; in other words, to discuss the methods of fly-fishing and bait-casting and other angling ways and means, as distinguished from the exclusive question of tackle. Every angler knows that good tackle is half the battle—and only half.

Secondarily, it is hoped that the reproductions of the photographs may, at least, suggest the part which, with little difficulty and at no very great expense, the camera may be made to play in the angler's days on stream and lake.

The greater part of the following text and photographs have appeared in OUTING, *Recreation,* and *Country Life in America.* The author's thanks are hereby tendered the publishers of those periodicals for permission to use the material in the present form.

SAMUEL G. CAMP.

CANAAN, CONNECTICUT.

CONTENTS

	Page
THE BROOK TROUT AND THE FLY-CASTER....	1
The Lure of the Trout Pools.............	1
The Brook Trout	3
Fly-tackle	7
Stream Fly-fishing in General............	14
Some Brook Trout Eccentricities..........	20
FLY-FISHING FOR BROWN AND RAINBOW TROUT	24
The Brown Trout	24
The Rainbow Trout	34
FLY-FISHING THE MOUNTAIN BROOK, THE POOLS, AND STILL-WATERS...........	38
Small Stream Fishing...................	39
Fishing the Pools and Still-waters.........	46
Dry-fly Fishing	52
FLY-CASTING AND FLY-FISHING..............	56
How to Improve your Fly-casting........	57
How to Fish the Flies..................	65
THE BAIT-CASTER AND THE SWEET-WATER BASSES	73
The Natural History of the Black Bass....	74
Bait-casting Tackle	79
Casting from the Reel..................	83
Some Practical Suggestions...............	85
When the Bloom is off the Water........	87

CONTENTS (*Continued*)

	Page
THE NAMAYCUSH, THE MASCALONGE, AND OTHERS	95
Deep-trolling for the Great Lakes Trout	96
The Mascalonge, Pike, and Pickerel	106
The Ouananiche and Land-locked Salmon	112
FINE AND FAR-OFF FISHING AND OTHER MATTERS	119
Fishing Fine and Far Off	119
Casting for Accuracy, Delicacy, and Distance	126
How to Improve the Fly-rod	130
Strip-casting for Black Bass	136
PROSPECTING WITH A CASTING ROD	145
On the Trail of the Black Bass	145
Fishing New Waters	147
CASTS AT RANDOM WITH UNEXPECTED RISES	155
The Wideawake Angler	155
Game Fish in Winter	159
In a Fishing Camp	165
Canoe *vs.* Waders	167
Landing Net and Gaff	169
The Trolling and Casting Spoon	172
The Way of a Trout with a Fly	174

THE BROOK TROUT AND THE FLY-CASTER

CHAPTER I

THE BROOK TROUT AND THE FLY-CASTER

The Lure of the Trout Pools.

FLY-FISHING for the speckled brook trout has a hold upon its votaries such as no other outdoor sport can boast. The interest of your simon-pure fly-fisherman in his pastime is more than a mere matter of the open season, it is lasting and ever present. He is a crank on the subject and proud of the title. If you disagree with him as to the status of the sport he will decline to argue the question with you—ignorance so colossal as yours is not to be met with arguments. He is simply sorry for you. And yet, no matter what may be your opinion of fly-casting as a sport, you cannot but envy him. The reasons for this supreme contentment and enviable absorption are, however, although of the very best, somewhat difficult of explanation to the uninitiated.

Of course, to a certain extent, one can describe the typical trout stream. It is not a large stream; rather, a big brook or little river. Its banks are pleasantly wooded, with here and there a small clearing where one time some logging job extended to the water's edge. Alternately there are hurrying, turbulent rapids or shallow, clear, swift-running riffles and deep, opaque pools whose surfaces reflect the pines and hemlocks and in whose depths the aldermen of the river repose in dignified inertia. Occasionally there are falls where the stream foams down many feet in a graceful, white, outbending ribbon. And again there are long, still reaches where the current is scarcely perceptible and where, if you would land a trout, you must indeed cast "fine and far off."

But no word-picture of the characteristics of the trout stream portrays in the slightest degree the characteristics of that same stream from the fly-fisherman's point of view. While he is fully aware of the natural beauties of the stream, the angler is apt to regard it more or less technically. And in this technicality of viewpoint, difficult in itself to define, lies the still greater difficulty of explaining the true relation of the stream to the stream fisherman.

One can also describe the fly-caster's tackle; the graceful, resilient split-bamboo; the delicate yet, when well selected, steel-strong lines and leaders; and the various flies, each having its special connotation for the experienced fly-caster. But these comprise merely the mechanical part of the game. The operation of casting the fly may also be explained, but this, too, is purely mechanical. However, in the skilful handling of fine tackle lies a large part of the angler's enjoyment.

I am inclined to believe that fly-fishing has its chief and most easily defined excuse in the existence of a certain game fish—*Salvelinus fontinalis,* the speckled brook trout. Here, indeed, is something tangible, a thing which may be taken in the hand—first catch your trout—and looked upon. No one seeing a freshly caught brook trout would say that it was other than a thing of beauty. Its delicate, vari-colored resplendency is not equaled by any living thing. The tarpon—Silver King of Southern waters—the Atlantic and Pacific salmons, the ouananiche and land-locked salmon, and the grayling comprise practically all the other game fishes, excepting the various other forms of brook trout, which may be said to possess both beauty of form and coloration.

The Brook Trout.

It cannot be denied that these fish are justifiably praised, but it is generally conceded that the red-spotted brook trout has nothing to fear from their competition. Of the Western trout, the rainbows, cutthroats, and steelheads, the rainbow, *Salmo irideus,* is the Eastern brook trout's nearest competitor—and that is praise enough for the rainbow. So here is one good reason, at least, why fly-fishing for trout is considered by many the very best of all sports.

But, after all, the lure of the trout pools is a thing intangible, elusive, which cannot be crystallized into so many words, or geometrically demonstrated. If you would solve its mysteries, would truly fathom the fascination of "the reek of the split-bamboo," you must hit the trail to a good trout stream, with fly-rod and camera, and there your desire will find its fulfilment—if you are the right sort; otherwise, otherwise.

While the Eastern brook trout is undoubtedly in coloration the most beautiful of all game fishes, in formation, especially as regards very large trout of, say, three pounds or over, its position is not so clearly first. The male trout of this weight, however finely marked with various tints of blue, crimson, and gold, tends dangerously to aldermanic girth and, with his usual under-shot and cruel lower jaw, is rather a creature to respect for gameness and fighting-blood than to admire artistically.

Coloration of Trout.

The quality of coloration in the brook trout, too, is dependent to a great extent upon the immediate surroundings affected by the fish. That this is a matter of protective coloration should go without gainsaying. In very dark waters, well shaded and with muddy or darkly colored bottom, the brook trout is sympathetically of subdued coloration, sometimes almost black—a very dark purple. On the other hand, in clear streams running over white gravel or pebbly beds, the trout are lightly tinted and often have a golden luster or sheen that is unequaled for beauty. The wise men tell us that variation of color in brook trout is caused by the light acting through the nerves of the eye upon certain color glands. It is also dependent to a certain extent upon the natural food most common to the stream, trout which have an abundance of insect food being the most brilliant in coloration as well as the largest.

To catch trout with the fly it is not at all necessary

to know that, as a matter of scientific fact, the brook trout is not a trout but a charr. Briefly, as regards the *Salmonidae,* the books of authority recognize the salmon trout and the charr trout, the distinction being founded upon the fact that the charrs have no teeth upon the front of the bone in the roof of the mouth, the contrary being the case with the salmon trout. Of the charrs those most familiar to the angler are the Great Lakes trout, *Cristivomer namaycush,* the "Namaycush," and *fontinalis, Salvelinus* meaning "little charr." In this connection it might be well to say that the trout of British angling literature is not our common native trout but the brown trout, *Salmo fario,* now pretty generally introduced into this country and a true trout, not a charr.

The Brook Trout a Charr.

The brook trout, although found in many lakes, is essentially a creature of running waters highly aerated and of low temperature, sixty-five degrees being about the highest temperature consistent with their continued existence and welfare. So, in a way, the speckled trout is a neighbor of the ruffed grouse, the white-tailed deer, and the gray squirrel, living in forest and woodland streams, spring born and fed, where the water, running between wooded banks, is shaded and cool, and the many waterfalls and rocky riffles afford air in abundance.

The Brook Trout at Home.

The appeal of trout fly-fishing to the sportsman is due in great part to the mere fact that "going to the woods" is inseparably connected with the best of the sport. The man who for a day, or many days, wades down a secluded trout stream, not so intent upon his cast of flies as to fail in observation of his surroundings, or to miss the many chance meetings with the furred and feathered forest dwellers so frequently offered the angler who has the faculty of seeing, is never dissatisfied with his "luck"; his days upon the stream, be the creel light or heavy, the Red Gods propitious or otherwise, are always the most pleasant of memories, to be dreamed again by the winter fireside and repeated at the earliest opportunity.

About the spawning habits of trout, it may be that some time when walking through the woods in the autumn, possibly hunting ruffed grouse or deer, you will come upon some little mountain stream. If you ever do and will take the pains to look for them, you may see some very fine trout in that inconsequential rivulet. In October and November, the temperature of the water having its influence over the exact time, the brook trout may be found at the headwaters of the streams and up the little "feeder" brooks where the spawning takes place. The female constructs the nest, brushing away the sand and gravel with nose and tail so as to form a slight depression in the stream bed, and the eggs are deposited therein. The male trout, at this time of exceptionally high and brilliant coloration, is in constant attendance. The brook trout, however, unlike the black bass, when the spawning is completed gives the nest no further attention. Under natural conditions, as distinguished from fish cultural results, only a very small

Spawning Habits.

percentage of the eggs are hatched, possibly, at best, five per cent. The time of incubation is from sixty to ninety days.

Growth and Range. Under favorable circumstances it takes about three years to make a pound trout, but the extent of the waters inhabited and the abundance or lack of food therein—also the nature of the food supply—have great influence in determining the rate of growth of brook trout. As above noted they thrive best upon insect food. The range of the brook trout is quite extensive; for instance, they may be found in nearly all of the United States, although they are not indigenous to all of the States whose waters they now inhabit. As to the numbers in which they may be found in any given locality, it is well, when planning a fishing trip, to remember that often, as Henry Guy Carleton has said, the brook trout exists only "in the clear, cold, running prospectus of a hotel charging $4 a day."

Fly-tackle

The tackle for trout fly-fishing has been developed to a point of excellence where further improvement, save in unimportant details, seems impossible. The rods, reels, lines, and flies now specially made for the fly-caster are certainly things of beauty and, if carefully treated, practically permanent joys. The matter of tackle selection for brook trout fly-fishing is a very simple affair—to the man who knows. But the man who does not know is quite capable of going to considerable expense for a museum of tackle curiosities the collective intent of which would be difficult to determine.

Herein it will be possible to state only with the utmost brevity compatible with clearness the essential tools and tackle of the fly-caster. For a more detailed treatise on fly-tackle and general equipment the reader is referred to "Fishing Kits and Equipment" by the present writer. Many years of stream use and experiment have shown that only certain tools are suited to effective and satisfactory—and sportsmanlike—fly-casting. In the following the suitability of the outfit to stream wading and fly-fishing in an average trout stream is primarily considered.

To the absolute exclusion of every other material the fly-rod should be of split-bamboo. The split-cane rod **The Fly-rod.** alone has the necessary speed and resilience which are imperative for effective and comfortable fly-casting and fly-fishing. Solid wood rods of either lancewood, greenheart, or bethabara are very much slower in action than the split-bamboo, and the steel rod is not at all to be considered. It should be said, however, that in the cheaper grades the split-bamboo rod is inferior to the solid wood rod of equal price. The angler should select a fly-rod of either medium or, if the purse is a fairly long one, the very best grade. A good fly-rod is worth every cent you pay for it—and more; also it should be said that good tackle of any sort is not only its own reward but is absolutely essential if you would have the best of the sport. Shoddy tackle conduces to careless work on the stream and consequently to poor success. On the other hand, good tackle tends to interest one in its proper handling, both in casting and also in fishing the flies, and as a result the angler finds his interest and success increasing rather than otherwise.

Choice must be made between the six-strip and eight-strip rods, the split-bamboo rod being made from triangular strips—usually six or eight—rent from the natural cane and cemented and bound together. Expert opinion favors the six-strip fly-rod.

If the angler is to have but one rod probably ten feet is the best length, but any length from nine to ten feet is generally satisfactory. It depends a great deal upon the character of the waters to be fished. For small brooks the shorter rod is preferable, but for big, rough streams where long casting must be done and large trout handled in swift water the ten-foot rod is best.

Be sure to have the ferrules and reel-seat of the rod of German silver. This material is stronger, cleaner, and more serviceable than nickeled brass. The hand-grasp should be of the sort known in the tackle trade as "solid cork," not a mere sheathing of composition-cork over a wooden form. For fly-casting the reel-seat must be below the hand-grasp. The guides of the rod should by all means be of the pattern known as English "snake" guides, and their material should be steel or German silver, the former being most suitable because the line will not wear grooves in them as in the softer German silver.

Select a rod that bends equally from handgrasp to tip-end, one that balances well—is not either tip or butt heavy—and is not too limber or whippy. The whippy rod is a poor caster and one with which it is difficult to hook and play a fish properly. Fly-rods from nine to ten feet in length should weigh from five to six and a quarter ounces.

The only reel for fly-casting is a simple single-action click reel. Because of its construction it is free from line-fouling, wherein it differs much from the multipliers when used in fly-casting. Multiplying reels have an outstanding balance-handle which continually interferes with the line when the latter is used in the proper way for casting the fly. The single-action reel has a protecting-band around the side plate, within which the handle revolves, thus almost entirely obviating line-fouling. The one-hundred yard reel is a very good size, and hard rubber and German silver in combination are serviceable and satisfactory reel materials. The larger sizes of the single-action reels must be used to hold the necessary amount of enameled line.

The Single-action Reel.

The next requisite is twenty-five yards of waterproof enameled silk line. For the nine-foot rod a line of size F is right; for the ten-foot rod, size E. No attempt should be made to use any other sort of line. The enameled line alone has the weight and smoothness necessary for good casting; it will not foul by wrapping around the rod. Good casting is impossible when using a light line on a heavy rod or vice versa. In fly-casting the reel should be used underneath the rod with the handle to the right.

The Right Line for Fly-casting.

Quite naturally two of the most important items in a

fly-fishing outfit are the fly-book and its contents. To select intelligently the flies upon which your
Trout Flies. success or non-success will very greatly depend it is necessary to take into consideration a number of facts known to be generally applicable. As a general rule avoid brilliant flies; flies of subdued coloration, except in wilderness streams where the trout will take anything, are practically the only successful ones. Upon very dark days, or when the water is slightly flooded and discolored, they should be lighter in color and somewhat larger than those used when both weather and water are clear.

Flies of numbers eight, ten, and twelve, are generally the best, number eight being the most universally effective, although late in the season, or at any time when the stream is very low and clear, numbers ten and twelve and occasionally even smaller are to be preferred. Personally I would be satisfied with the following trout flies in good quantity and range of sizes: coachman, grizzly king, cowdung, Cahill, Beaverkill, queen of the water, brown hackle, Montreal, and March brown.

A great deal depends upon the hooks on which the flies are dressed. The Sproat hook, all things considered, is much the best. Above all things avoid cheap flies; they are flimsily tied upon hooks of poor quality and are far more deceiving to the tyro fly-fisher than to the brook trout. It is a very good plan to use the coachman, a consistently successful fly at all times and seasons, for your end fly. The white wing of this fly is easily seen in broken water, and sometimes when using small, dark colored flies in the rapids it is almost impossible to tell just where the cast is. A good strong fly-book to hold at least four dozen flies is necessary.

In addition to the flies named above the angler planning a trip to the famous trout waters of Maine and Canada, the Rangeleys, the Nepigon, and other lakes and large streams should add to his collection the Parmachene belle (first tied by Henry P. Wells, the writer of that best of all fly-fishing books, "Fly-rods and Fly-tackle," with a special view to use in Maine waters) and the silver doctor upon hooks of larger sizes than those above suggested; it should be stated, however, that even in wilderness streams flies dressed on small hooks are often the only successful ones. The last named flies are also good for sea trout and ouananiche.

Latterly American anglers are taking up to some extent the English method of dry-fly casting, using a floating fly which is always cast dry and fished upon the surface of the water—a very effective method for fishing still-waters and large, quiet pools. It does not seem advisable to discuss dry-fly fishing at this point, since we are now speaking only generally of fly-fishing methods. Dry-fly fishing is an extremely specialized form of the sport and is described in a later chapter on "Fishing the Pools and Still-waters."

Other fly-fishing requisites are leaders, leader box, creel, landing net, and waders. On the trout fly-rod leaders longer than six feet should not generally be used on account of the danger of reeling the leader knot through the tip-guide and thus locking the line fast.

The six-foot leader is best for three flies; when using two flies, the preferable number, a five-foot leader is sufficiently long. Select the size known as "medium trout." The choice of leaders, however, is intimately connected, both as to length and caliber, with the stage of water and weather conditions. Longer and finer leaders must be used over low, clear water than when fishing the stream under normal conditions. Leaders must never be used when dry and brittle and must first be soaked in water to render them pliable; for this purpose the angler should carry two or three leaders in a nickel leader box between layers of wet felt.

Other Trout Fishing Duffle.

A nine-pound creel, with "new style" shoulder sling leaving the casting arm free, is most suited to average trout fishing in streams. In the matter of waders it may be said that for general purposes light-weight hip-boots are about as good as any. Late in the season it is the best plan to do without waders and wear regular wading shoes, with canvas leggings, or any pair of shoes with small slits cut in them to let out the water. Light-weight knee-high hunting boots are very satisfactory for this purpose; they should be well oiled. Hob-nails not too many, too hard, or too large, are advantageous when wading very rocky streams.

A small landing net which may be slung over the shoulder by an elastic cord, or fitted with a catch so that it may be hung on a button or ring on the front of the coat, should always be carried; the angler who religiously packs a landing net will far less frequently tell the familiar story of the "whale" that "got away."

To be sure, a landing net is more or less of a nuisance in the brush, but it should be considered as a very necessary evil. Late in the season fly-medicine or "dope" is a necessary item; frequently, as I have said elsewhere, it spells the difference between fly-fishing and mere fly-fighting. A canvas, khaki, or duxbak hunting coat because of its many pockets is handiest for trout fishing wear and very durable. The waterproof quality of the duxbak material is especially desirable.

Stream Fly-fishing in General

The typical trout stream of the woodlands or wilderness, as intimated above, is a thing of infinite variety. Swift-running, shallow riffles deepen and increase in swiftness, forming strong, turbulent rapids. These are succeeded by falls, and at the foot are dark, quiet pools. Now one comes upon some long, still reach where there is little or no current; and again he finds the stream combining riffle and quiet water in a manner difficult to describe.

The stream bed is also subject to constant variation. Although in most trout streams gravel bottom predominates, yet there will be many places where it will be merely sand, possibly large boulders lying close together, or perhaps the bottom will be weedy. You know there are trout in the stream—but where? Are they in the riffles, rapids, or pools? What is the nature of the stream bottom for which they may have some passing preference? Obviously the solution is a matter of natural history—the habits of the brook trout.

The brook trout is essentially a creature of varied moods and tenses. He is here to-day; gone to-morrow. To-day he favors some certain fly, to-morrow another and quite different insect. At one time he is lively and playful; at another sluggish and sulky. To an uncertain degree only can his actions be forecasted. But, although he is eccentric, and many of his actions are exceptions to all rules, several facts are generally true of him. Given the proper outfit and competent skill in its use, there remains for the fly-fisherman only the necessity of compassing as far as may be these general truths about trout.

In October or November trout ascend to the headwaters of the streams for the purpose of spawning. Then they drift gradually back to lower waters, and early spring finds them in the pools and deeper portions of the stream. At this time the water is usually bank-high and full of "snow-broth." Even after the snow has disappeared from the immediate vicinity of the river snow-water is still running, for in the deep mountain ravines from which the little "feeder" brooks flow down ice and snow remain until the season is well advanced. Thus early in the season trout are torpid and when hooked show little or no spirit. As soon as the river is fairly clear they will take bait, and this is the most successful way of fishing for them at this time.

Early Fishing.

If you insist on fly-fishing you can hope for only moderate returns. The trout are ground-feeding and rise to the surface with the utmost reluctance. One method of fly-fishing under these conditions is to use a silver doctor or some other brilliantly colored fly and fish it well beneath the surface. The shining, silver body of this fly has a minnow-like glitter when drawn through the water that will sometimes induce a fish to strike. But, all things considered, it is far better to depend on your bait-box, or, if you are a fly-fishing purist, to stay at home. Most of us consider it a sacred duty to wet a line on the opening day or as soon thereafter as possible. This duty fulfilled, we are content to await the more favorable conditions which prevail in May and June.

When the stream has resumed its normal level and clarity and the water has been warmed by the spring sunshine, the fly-fishing is at its best. Insect life is now abundant on the banks and over the surface of the water. The fish are in the riffles and rapids, having deserted the deeper pools and reaches. Also, they are constantly foraging and their taste in the matter of insects, both natural and artificial, is much more catholic than later in the season. Other things being equal, the fly-fisherman is now in his glory and should have no difficulty in making a good score.

Mid-season Fishing.

Then comes the late spring and summer fishing. Now, indeed, must one cast fine and far-off. Low and clear water prevails. The hot sun for weeks has beaten on the stream, and the trout, seeking the cool water which their nature demands, are again in the deeper waters, about the spring-holes, and generally farther up-stream than theretofore. You may find the lower portions of the

Late Fishing.

stream practically trout deserted. A good place to cast, at this time, is where some little mountain brook empties into the river. Fishing in the early morning and late afternoon is the most resultful. In the cool of the evening the trout work out from their day-time lairs and may be found feeding in the riffles.

With the above generalities as a basis we can now consider with more detail certain special aspects of the trout problem. In trout fishing, as in many other things, it is a good plan to make haste slowly. One can never tell with certainty just where the fish may be lying. Until you have arrived at some reasonable conclusion on this point, fish all the water. Try the little, shallow ripples near the banks. Wet the flies in every part of the riffles and rapids. When you come to a pool fish all of it from the head, then go around and fish all of it from below. Do not neglect the little eddies around boulders and half-submerged trees. Many times the best fish are taken in the most unlikely places.

Where to Look for Trout.

Where the stream has fretted away the soil so as to form a hiding place beneath the overhanging bank, watch out for the "big one." Proceeding in this manner, you will soon discover the nature of the places where the majority of the fish are lying, and if your time is limited you can pass by those which seem least productive. On some days most of the trout will be found in the riffles; on others the riffles are deserted by all save the smallest fry and you will strike most of your trout in the deeper rapids or the pools.

In the experimental stage of the day's fishing it is

Casting Experiments. well also to determine as quickly as possible which method of presenting the flies seems to be most popular with the fish. If the customary method of casting, that is, keeping the flies well up on the surface, does not produce sufficiently satisfactory results, try the submerged fly. A variation in the method frequently spells the difference between success and failure. I have often made good baskets of trout by fishing the flies from six inches to a foot underneath the surface, when, at the same time, it was impossible to induce a strike by orthodox surface fishing.

Trout habits are in great measure a matter of locality. If you are to fish a stream that is new to you, by all means get into communication, if possible, with some local angler and believe all that he tells you. If he is the right kind of a sportsman he will save you many hours which might otherwise be spent in unsuccessful experimenting.

Practical Hints. Down-stream fishing is best adapted to the swift current of most American trout streams, although where the stream is quiet it may properly, and sometimes to better advantage, be fished "up." Large, quiet pools and extensive still-waters may properly first be whipped at the lower part and then from the head. It is not at all necessary to be early on the stream; there are more natural flies on the water after the sun has been up for a time and consequently the trout are then more likely to rise to the artificials. Early in the season a bright day is no disadvantage, rather the opposite; but later, in the latter part of June and in summer, an overcast day is far the best.

Other things being equal, the angler who is most skilled in striking his fish will have a much heavier creel than the one less proficient in this respect. To connect consistently with rising trout demands cool nerves and the quickest of eyes and wrist. The strike must come at just the proper time and with just the proper degree of force. The too strenuous strike will tear the hook away from the fish.

It is a better fault to strike too quickly than too late. If you strike too quickly the trout will be missed clean and not pricked, and will often rise again, but if the strike is delayed and the fish has the chance to mouth the fly he will instantly eject it and will certainly not rise again. Strike with the wrist only at the first suspicion of a rising fish—you can hardly strike too quickly—and with a degree of force in proportion to your tackle and the trout; large trout should be struck good and hard. In the rapids trout will often hook themselves; it is when fishing the still pools and reaches of quiet water that skilled striking is at a premium.

Do not hurry about landing the fish. Let him run, always keeping a taut line and steering him away from the danger spots, until he is pretty well played out; then lead him to the landing net in some quiet side eddy, or beach him on some sloping bar. When using the net have it submerged and lead the fish over it. To do this effectively you should be down-stream from the fish so that the current will float the fish over the net instead of away from it.

Always line your creel with wet moss or ferns to keep the trout fresh and looking as if newly caught.

Always kill your fish immediately after taking him off the hook, and when you are wading the rapids it is a wise plan to kill him before you take him off. Medium-sized trout may be killed easily by inserting the forefinger or thumb in the mouth and bending the head sharply backward.

Brook Trout Eccentricities. That the brook trout is most eccentric in its habits is generally conceded. Whether it is more finicky than the black bass is a question, for this fish, also, is famous for its uncertainties. The man who "knows all about trout" does not exist, although you have probably met him. Long experience in trout fishing, both with fly and bait, is conducive to a deeply rooted belief that the brook trout will most certainly not "stay put." When you think you have pinned him down as to some phase of character or habit, your next fishing trip is quite apt to result in a complete reversal of opinion as to that same characteristic.

Experts agree to disagree, and arguments concerning *fontinalis* are unending and profitable only in that they serve to sustain angling interest. Not only is there confusion as to these matters of character and habit, but the scientists meet with more difficulty in dealing with the *Salmonidae* than with any other group of game fishes. With elusive ease and supreme indifference the trout refuse to be classified and ichthyologically tagged. As to this, however, the fisherman need not concern himself over-much, since he has his own troubles.

In stream fishing, for instance, it frequently happens that after a run of good luck the fish suddenly cease rising and are apparently down to stay. The angler who faces this situation is usually hopelessly at sea. The question of what to do obstinately remains unanswered. It may be that some temporary hatch of flies upon which the trout have been feeding has ceased. It may be that that particular stretch of water is temporarily deserted by the trout for some unknown reason. Perhaps this portion of the river is permanently avoided by the fish. Explanations and theories buzz merrily in the angler's brain, and finally he "goes it blind."

At every few casts he changes flies. He tries both surface and submerged fishing. Without avail he employs every fly-fishing artifice known to him. At last, when he is discouraged and about to take the rod down, he gets a rise and a trout. Then another candidate appears and is elected to the creel. Exactly what has happened the angler does not know, and, since the fish are again on the rise, he cares little until home again and in conversation with some fellow fisherman the occurrence is brought up for argument and thoroughly sifted. Generally some sufficiently plausible explanation is concocted and confidently relied upon until a similar state of affairs arises on a subsequent trip and the pet theory suffers a compound fracture.

One of the most exasperating of trout habits is that of rising short. When the fish are in this mood the angler's character suffers in inverse ratio to his capacity for patient endurance under much adversity. Whether it is a matter for congratulation that when the trout are rising short they are generally rising pretty freely is a question. Certainly the more short rises you have, with consequent failures to hook the fish, the more you are inclined to wax exceeding wroth and feel like smashing things. But this free rising of the fish, even under these conditions, generally results in a capture now and then, and for this reason it should probably be considered a good rather than an evil.

When the fish are acting in this manner the angler is at first inclined to believe that he is striking too quickly and jerking the flies away. But if he steadies down and strikes more deliberately, he soon discovers that the fault is with the fish. To increase his discomfiture it generally happens that the trout strikes just closely enough to result in being pricked and lost.

So far as the writer knows there is no remedy. It is simply to be endured. The exact mental bias of a brook trout when he is determined to rise short has been variously conjectured, but is still to be definitely decided. It has been claimed that he is merely playful; that he desires to maim the insect for future reference, or, perhaps for the fun of the cruelty; also, that he rises purely out of curiosity and without intention or desire to take the lure. Any of these theories is probable, plausible, and possible, and the angler may take his choice with the certainty that whichever of them he may elect to rely upon may be easily proved conclusively—and with equal ease absolutely discredited.

Probably the most heartrending situation with which

the trout fly-fisherman is now and again confronted is when the trout are jumping continually, feeding upon some certain fly, or, it may be, in play. At such times the angler's desire to obtain a few "specimens" of the brook trout is greatly increased by the sight of the leaping fish, while at the same time, if he is an experienced angler, he is fully aware of the fact that no possible conditions could be more unpropitious for success. Very rarely it will happen that if the trout are rising to some natural fly the angler can make a killing by hitting upon the most approximate artificial. It seldom occurs. The right fly, somehow, is hardly ever in the fly-book. Here again the angler realizes his utter helplessness, and very acutely.

The whys and wherefores of the brook trout are innumerable and as unsolvable as numerous. To the sportsman they are a never-ending source of interest and of difficulty. The wise angler will thank Heaven each time he creels a trout—it may be the very last one.

CHAPTER II

FLY-FISHING FOR BROWN AND RAINBOW TROUT

WHEN the Eastern angler speaks of fly-fishing for trout the speckled brook trout, *Salvelinus fontinalis,* is always implied; but while it is true that, fortunately, the red-spotted trout is still the most common resident of our streams, yet in many streams *fontinalis* now shares the water with one or both of two other good game fishes, the brown trout and the rainbow trout, *Salmo fario* and *Salmo irideus* respectively. Of the two the brown trout is the more common and it is well for the fly-caster to know something about its nature and habits and the most suitable tackle and methods for fly-fishing for brown trout; also he should know the facts of a similar nature regarding the rainbow.

The Brown Trout

Notwithstanding the fact that the brown trout had been a resident of many of our streams for a good many years, to be exact since 1882, it seems that among anglers in general exact information concerning this trout is rather difficult to find. To one who has had the opportunity and privilege of taking this fish in goodly numbers the dissertations, opinions, disputes, and theories of fishermen who have not enjoyed a close acquaintance with *Salmo fario,* but are ever ready to discuss the subject, are somewhat amusing.

To cite a concrete example: Recently a reasonably proficient angler, journeying from one of our larger cities to a trout stream which the writer has fished times almost innumerable, brought home with him a number of strange, outlandish fish all very sizable. The angler stated to an admiring audience of friends that the fish had fought like tigers, that he had had the time of his life, etc., etc.—but what were they? Briefly, the fish were imagined to be of every sort except the right one, and some of the guesses were particularly wild and humorous. The fish were simply brown trout.

It is the purpose of this chapter to state some of the facts known to many anglers about the brown trout and, it would seem, quite unknown to many others, possibly to the majority. First, however, the writer would recall the somewhat trite fact that comparisons are always and inevitably odious. Wherefore, one might suggest that our native trout be left out of the discussion. For some reason unknown to the present writer, anglers are prone at the very mention of the brown trout to consider the entire question one of comparison between the brown and the native, naturally to the detriment of the former; *fontinalis vs. fario* has been argued times without number.

Fontinalis vs. Fario.

The discussion is futile. Rightly, there can be no question as regards the respective sporting qualities of the two. Our native trout, the speckled brook trout, is clearly in a class by itself. No other trout, or any other game fish, has ever been or ever will be so well beloved by sportsmen. So let us consider the brown trout strictly on its own merits and not as an actual or even possible rival of our red-spotted charr.

The German or brown trout was first planted in American waters, as above noted, in 1882, the eggs coming from Germany and England. **Origin in America.** For some time thereafter the fish were propagated and planted by the United States Bureau of Fisheries, but at the present time fry or fingerlings can only be obtained from private hatcheries. The Federal Bureau ceased distributing the brown trout for reasons which will appear later. Before the cessation of propagation, however, the range of the brown trout had attained large proportions, and they are now to be found in very many of our trout streams both East and West.

The brown trout is a true trout, a salmon trout, and not a charr, in which it differs from our native trout. If you are a good angler and kill your **The Brown Trout a True Trout.** fish immediately after landing them—which, as suggested in the preceding chapter, can best be done in the case of trout of moderate size by inserting the forefinger in the mouth of the fish and bending the head sharply backward—you will have reason to note very "sharply" an anatomical difference between the mouth of a salmon trout and that of a charr. The brown trout has teeth in no uncertain quantity or degree of penetration on the front of the bone in the roof of the mouth. These are lacking in the charr. It should be said also that the presence of this efficient dental weapon at once marks the brown trout as a fish killer.

A good many years ago I caught my first brown trout, a rather small specimen, and although at the time I did not know the exact nature of **Coloration.** the fish, it was evident at once that it was no very close relative of our common trout—simply because the fish had very appreciable scales. The scales of our native trout, although they exist, are microscopic. Those of the brown trout are easily seen. The coloration of the brown trout is quite different from that of any other trout either native, rainbow, or any of the Western species. The color scheme is best described by William C. Harris, as follows:

"The brown trout is, in American waters, rather slimmer in build than our American red-spotted trout, with a larger and more pointed head. The back is dark green covered with well-defined black spots, and the dorsal fin has both black and bright red or vermilion spots; the adipose, or fatty fin, is also beautifully decorated with three red spots. Below the lateral line the coloration is of a yellowish cast with a greenish silvery background. The tail, or caudal fin, is square, and on its edges there is a reddish stripe; the other fins are orange in color, the ventral and anal having a white stripe on the under edge shaded with deep orange; the head, the under part of which is yellow, and the gill covers are covered with dark spots; the belly is pure white, above which is a deep yellow hue."

The back of the brown trout is not marbled, or vermiculated, as in the case of *fontinalis*. The coloration is quite as susceptible to change due to environment as that of the native trout. The most beautiful specimens are those living in fast water, unshaded, and running over gravel bottom. Such fish are extremely brilliant in coloration, with vivid red spots and a very beautiful golden luster. Others, living in slow, deep, shaded water with dark bottom, are dull in coloration. The spawning period and habits are practically those of the native trout.

The Brown Trout and the Dry-fly. The brown trout is *the* trout of our English brother anglers and is the fish either particularly referred to or implied as a matter of course in the English literature of fly-fishing. Over there the pursuit of the trout—the Britisher takes his sport rather more seriously than does the Yankee—has been reduced to an exact science, at least to such a degree of exactness as the nature of the sport permits. The outcome of this determined onslaught upon the ranks of the brown trout is seen in the resultant English method of dry-fly fishing, latterly coming into some prominence in this country. A single dry or floating fly is used, and cast only —in case the angler is a dry-fly purist, that is, in the last stages of the disease—to a rising trout. The artificials mostly in use are exact imitations of the prevalent insect life of the stream.

The reports of American anglers who have experimented with the dry-fly on home waters are not, on the whole, over-enthusiastic, although in individual cases some very remarkable successes have been recorded. The paucity of results may be due, although I have never seen it suggested, to the characteristic difference between the native and the brown trout. The dry-fly method has been evolved almost purely as a means of taking the latter, and it seems not unreasonable that an effective method for taking the one should fail somewhat in the case of the other. Dry-fly fishing should be entirely successful on any suitable American stream abounding in brown trout, for, although there are slight variations of habit between the brown trout of British and those of American streams, they are not of such a degree or nature as to render it probable that a method so successful on the other side should be much less effective here. But the water must be suitable; that is, not too swift and broken.

Purely as a sporting proposition the brown trout is a decided success. In other words, he puts up a good fight. There are marked differences, **Fighting Qualities.** however, between the way a brown trout conducts himself when taking a fly and thereafter and the behavior of the native. Especially noteworthy is the fact that very often the brown trout will leap on a slack line. Artists who illustrate the sportsmen's periodicals are fond of picturing the brook trout leaping high in the air with all the ease and athletic ability of the small-mouthed black bass, the Atlantic salmon, or the tarpon, but the observant and experienced reader, although he may condone the matter as merely poetic or artistic license, knows full well that the thing is a pure nature fake.

The brook trout, unless fairly yanked from the water by too strenuous rod work, so seldom that one can almost say positively never leaps from the water. In rare instances he may leap upon a slack line, but the general rule is quite the other way. The brook trout does not belong to that class of game fishes which may be called the leapers, but the brown trout may rightly be thus classified. The leap of the brown in the effort to rid himself of the hook is very much like that of the black bass, a spectacular and vicious shaking of the entire body in the air. I once struck a good rise of brown trout, taking six in almost that number of casts, running from a half to one pound, and every one of them jumped one or more times.

There is an impression that the brown trout rises reluctantly to the artificial fly. Nothing could be more erroneous. They are very free risers when conditions are at all favorable—quite as much so as the native trout. The fight of the brown trout is not as fast, as electric, as that of the native trout, but when in good condition the brownie is a very bulldog for tenacity, making a prolonged and decided objection to coming to the net. In fact, sometimes it is pretty hard to tell just when he is "all in"—it is a very hard fish to tire entirely out. Frequently when you have a brown trout of good fighting size almost at the edge of your landing net he will apparently acquire an entirely new lease of life and fight his way back to mid-stream.

As a general thing you will have little trouble in

hooking a large brown trout when he rises to the fly.

Striking. Striking is often quite unnecessary, for they take the fly in a very vicious and emphatic manner. A good many times the brown trout will leap from the water and take the fly on his downward flight. Usually the native does not show himself to any extent unless he misses the fly, when he will sometimes shoot straight up in the air. Of course, not every brown trout, or every speckled trout will conduct himself in this manner and in strict accordance with the general rules; the above states merely the general course of action of the two under normal conditions.

The brown trout should never be planted in a stream inhabited by native trout unless the conditions are such

Planting Brown Trout. that the natives are few and small and stocking with them does not materially improve the situation. The brown is a very fast grower and attains a large size, the increase being estimated at about one pound a year. Owing to the piscivorous nature of the brown trout and their larger size, natives and browns do not do well together, the former eventually yielding the stream to the foreigners. Disregard or ignorance of this fact when the brown trout was first introduced into this country is responsible in great part for the prejudice against them. But in streams no longer favorable to *fontinalis,* and there are many such due to logging operations, pollution, etc., the brown trout, by nature a hardier fish than our native charr, will still thrive, and such streams may be made to furnish good sport and a valuable food supply by stocking with brown trout. From imber operations results a rise in temperature in streams flowing through the affected tract. The brown trout thrives in water of a temperature that would be almost prohibitive to the existence of the native.

Very light tackle should not be used when fishing a stream wholly or partially inhabited by brown trout. The writer has seen many brownies weighing from two to three pounds, two fish weighing over four pounds each, and there are well authenticated captures of brown trout up to the vicinity of seven pounds. As noted below, the brown trout, when conditions are favorable, is a fast-water fish and even with reasonably strong though sportsmanlike tackle, the chances are very much in favor of the fish. The outfit should be strong throughout. A ten-foot six-ounce fly-rod is well suited to the game, and the leader particularly should be strong and of the finest quality.

Tackle for Brown Trout.

For wet-fly fishing any of the accepted trout flies, the choice being governed by the usual rules in regard to fly selection for the speckled trout, are effective, with a possible preference for the hackles; the gray hackle with red body is a particularly good brown trout fly. Large sized flies, on number six and four hooks, are occasionally very effective in deep, fast water. Reference has been made above to the utilization of dry-flies for fishing the pools and still-waters. As in the case of the brook trout the largest fish will most often be found in the pools. Many of the American stock trout flies may now be had dressed in dry-fly fashion,

BROWN AND RAINBOW TROUT

flies such as the Beaverkill, March brown, etc. A landing net is always a necessary and important factor on a brown trout water.

There seems to be a popular impression that the brown trout is essentially and by preference an inhabitant of slow, sluggish water. While it is true that the larger specimens are more apt to be found in the pools and deeper portions of the stream, coming to the shallows to feed at night—even as the native trout—it is still a fact that average fish, from a half-pound up to two pounds and a half, are most often found in the most broken, swift, and rocky water which the stream affords.

The Brownie a Fast-water Fish.

A peculiar fact, and one well worth noting, is that in such a reach of white water, the brown trout is very apt to lie on the upstream side of a boulder rather than in the lee below it, as would be generally true of the native trout. The discovery of this fact, very seldom true of the native trout, has been worth many good brown trout to the writer. The flies should be worked cross-current from three to six inches above and along the line where the water lips the boulder.

A Practical Fishing Hint.

The known presence of large trout in the stream lends an interest to a day's fly-fishing quite unknown when the angler is whipping a stream from which nothing over a half-pound is liable to be taken. A stream inhabited by brown trout has always this interesting possibility, while, unfortunately, the same cannot be

An Interesting Possibility.

said of the great majority of streams in which are native trout alone. Personally the writer confesses to a genuine admiration for the brown trout—with the conviction that he is not alone in this opinion, and also with the knowledge that many anglers have no use whatever for the brown trout—and, while still maintaining that our native brook trout is an unrivaled game fish, he is willing to give the devil his due; in other words, to declare that the brown trout is a game fish worth any angler's consideration and skill.

The Rainbow Trout

The rainbow trout, *Salmo irideus,* is far less common to Eastern trout streams than the brown trout; in the West the rainbow is indigenous to many streams. This is a true trout, a salmon trout and not a charr and, in fact, has more points in common with the brown trout than with the Eastern brook. It is a black-spotted trout; as in the case of the brown it will live in water of a higher temperature than will the native; it is famous for leaping when hooked, and is a faster grower than the native trout.

For some unknown reason stocking trout streams with rainbow fry or fingerlings is successful only in isolated cases. The common impression seems to be that the rainbows, if circumstances permit, desert the shallow water of the average trout stream and run down into deeper rivers and lakes. Whatever may be the reason, it is a fact that although many streams have been stocked with rainbows only a few of them are ever

Stocking with Rainbows.

taken on the rod and after a season or two they disappear entirely. But in some cases stocking with them has been entirely successful and the streams wherein they may be found afford some of the finest of flyfishing.

As a game fish there is no harder fighter than the rainbow. Almost invariably its first act when hooked is to leap high from the water; then follows a prolonged, fast-fought resistance sufficient to tax the skill of the most expert angler. The rainbow is a faster fighter than the brown trout, its quickness of movement resembling more the action of the native trout. The writer, however, has cause to remember his first rainbow for the reason that the fish did not leap—for good and sufficient reasons. Fishing at the confluence of two trout streams in very fast water where the currents of the two streams struggled for mastery, I hooked and after a running fight landed about a hundred yards downstream from that point a double consisting of a three-quarter pound rainbow and a native trout of one pound and a half. The native was taken on the end fly, a coachman, and the rainbow on the dropper, a Beaverkill. In this case the larger trout undoubtedly forced the fighting and held down the rainbow so that it was impossible for him to go into the air. Since then I have had numerous opportunities to admire the leaping and other sporting qualities of the rainbow.

As a Game Fish.

As to the distinctive coloration of the rainbow, William C. Harris whose writings, both as a practical angler and ichthyologist, on the natural history of game fish are authoritative and whom I have quoted above in connection with the brown trout, says:

Coloration of the Rainbow. "There are one species and five subspecies of the rainbows, the typical form being known as the rainbow or Coast Range trout (*Salmo irideus,* specific name from the Latin, 'a rainbow'). It is a large, robust, short, and deep fish, growing to a weight of thirteen pounds in the Williamson River, and up to thirty pounds when sea-run. The head is short, somewhat convex, and 'obtusely ridged above'; mouth slightly smaller than in other trout, and the eyes are somewhat larger; the teeth on the roof of the mouth are in two irregular series; the tail fin is slightly forked, the body, sides, and ventral fins irregularly but profusely marked with black spots, those on the tail being smaller than those on the body and on other fins.

"The coloration is bluish above and whitish on the sides, which also, in both sexes, have a broad lateral band with reddish blotches, the sea-run specimens being plain silvery. If an angler chances to catch a rainbow in Eastern waters, it will probably be where the Eastern brook trout is also found, and the 'red-sides' can easily be distinguished from it by the lateral band, more or less reddish, always on the sides of both sexes, and by the presence of numerous black irregular spots located on the body, head, and fins; those on the caudal fin being somewhat smaller than the spots elsewhere. The brook trout (*fontinalis*) has red spots; the rainbows do not have them."

The above description says that the rainbow is a "deep" fish, and that the "mouth is somewhat smaller than in other trout." Deep, here, is another way of saying narrow—the rainbow is very thin through the body, taking a half-pound specimen as an example—and it should be said also that the mouth is noticeably smaller than that of either the brown or native. While there is no room for argument as to the fighting qualities of the rainbow, in the writer's opinion and that of many other anglers the rainbow as an edible fish is not equal to either the native brook or brown trout. Another noticeable thing about the rainbow is the quickness with which the coloration fades after the fish is taken from the water; in a very short time the lateral band, the "rainbow," will almost entirely disappear, leaving only a faint suggestion of its natural beauty.

The rainbow is a very free riser to the artificial fly, apparently less discriminating in this respect than either native or brown trout. Any of the well-known fly patterns will be successful. In general the tackle advised for brown trout is equally suitable for fly-fishing for rainbows. The rainbow always seeks the swift water, grows to a larger size than the native trout, the rate of growth being about the same as that of the brown trout, and reasonably strong and efficient tackle is always best for heavy fish in heavy water.

Tackle.

CHAPTER III

FLY-FISHING THE MOUNTAIN BROOK, THE POOLS, AND STILL-WATERS

QUITE recently at the Upper Dam, Rangeley Lakes, Maine, "the place, of all others in the world, where the lunacy of angling may be seen in its incurable stage," a genuine brook trout, *fontinalis,* weighing twelve and a half pounds was captured. This trout, authenticated beyond doubt, was not taken by an angler but by some hatchery men for spawning purposes. At the same place, in the fall of 1908, a brook trout scaling nine pounds seven ounces was taken on the fly by Mr. Raymond S. Parrish, of Montville, Connecticut.

Some little time ago, at the biennial session of the General Assembly of a certain State, a bill came up for consideration making seven inches the length of trout to be legally retained. Whereupon the Honorable Member from—but that might identify the State—at any rate, the Honorable Member arose and, with tears in his eyes, protested that in his county, although there were several trout streams, many trout, and a well-established industry devoted to their capture, there

BROOKS, POOLS, STILL-WATERS

was not at that time in that county, or ever had been at any time in that county, a trout measuring seven inches. Wherefore the injustice of such a measure was palpable, etc., etc. The bill did not pass.

Trout fishing may mean one thing and it may mean another. It is a fact that in many parts of Vermont, Massachusetts, Connecticut, and other States, trout fishing such as that described by the Honorable Member is the rule and not the exception.

Small Stream Fly-fishing

Where average fishing may be had it is a very poor plan, one finely calculated to spoil sport, to fish the small mountain streams. These little brooks act as "feeders" for the larger streams and rivers. In the fall the trout of the larger streams ascend these little brooks to spawn and the little trout remain in them from the fry to the fingerling stage when they seek the deeper and more extensive streams. "Skinning" the small brooks merely means that the stock in the larger ones will surely deteriorate in numbers and in size, and eventually poor fishing or none at all will be the rule.

Do not Fish the Feeder Brook.

But if the small feeder brooks are religiously protected, the stocking of the larger streams is more or less automatic, no matter how hard these may be fished; this is especially true where the feeder brooks are stocked by the State or by individuals. It is manifestly futile to stock the small brooks and at the same time allow them to be fished. And stocking is most successful where the fry or fingerlings are planted in the tributary brooks where they are free from the large trout and the generally strenuous life of the river.

But where little brooks and small mountain trout are the rule and heavier fishing need not be taken into consideration, fly-fishing for the little charrs of the mountain streams is a legitimate sport—and not a half bad one.

A Legitimate Sport.

With trout fishing as, in fact, with any sport of the rod and gun, particularly in these days when light creels and hunting-coat pockets are the rule—the law in most localities jealously looking out for this—and the camera plays so important a part in field sports, the country to be fished or hunted, whether attractive or commonplace, is a primary consideration. It would be difficult to find a more pleasant field of action than that afforded by the typical mountain trout stream.

When you go fishing for mountain trout you seek the country of the ruffed grouse, the woodcock, the gray squirrel, and the white-tailed deer; withal, a somewhat strenuous country. Following the brook you pass through deep ravines strewn with green and moss-grown rocks, steep, slippery, moist, and prolific of mosquitoes, tumbles, tackle smash-ups—and trout. You work through little alder swamps, almost impenetrable tangles where there is nothing to see but the work ahead and nothing to do but do it—and catch trout. But, however difficult may be the local habitation of the mountain trout, it is sure to have the virtues of picturesqueness and freedom from monotony and to

Where the Mountain Trout Lives.

BROOKS, POOLS, STILL-WATERS

offer many opportunities for the camera as well as the rod.

Working quietly along the little stream you will sometimes flush a "partridge" and will often hear them drumming. Later in the spring a woodcock will perhaps get up within rod's length of you and whistle away over the tops of the alders. Where deer are at all common you will see their tracks along the brook and, if you are at all lucky—and quiet—you may even see the trail-makers. Incidents of this sort, with fair success with the little fly-rod, will surely serve to make your day on the stream a pleasant one. In such streams a trout weighing half a pound is a monster, and the average is considerably less than that. But sport with any game fish is largely a matter of the tackle used, and presumably you will use light tackle.

The little trout of the mountain streams, unless in very secluded brooks which have been fished little or not at all, are not in the least foolish or uneducated. Anglers are wont to associate extreme sophistication with the two-pounders of the big rivers. When considering the typical mountain trout it is well to remember that with them size is small indication of age or degree of education. The size of brook trout is a matter of range extent and food supply, and the trout of the little brooks of the hill country are small because the food supply is limited, the "swim" is limited, and the little fellows have to work hard for a living. So the eight-incher of the narrow, shallow, and rapid mountain stream may be as highly educated as the two-pound brown trout

Educated Trout.

which, in a more extensive stream, rises only to the fly cast "dry and cocked." At any rate, if you find a well-worn angler's path along the little stream you will have to use some finesse and no little patience and ingenuity to make a very heavy showing.

Fly-fishing for mountain trout has its technique equally with the sport on larger streams and weightier fish. The primary essential for success and sport is light tackle—the very lightest. Fly-casting in any true sense of the words is out of the question because of the confined and brushy nature of the stream. So the tackle need not be selected with a view to casting any considerable distance; this permits the use, since weight is unnecessary, of a small caliber line. An enameled line, size G, is exactly the thing. This may properly be used on a little four-ounce fly-rod eight feet in length or thereabouts. A very small single-action reel, the smaller the better, should be used, since it will not foul in the brush as often as a larger one.

Mountain Stream Fly-Tackle.

A very good plan is to wind on an additional guide between each pair of guides on the rod when much brush fishing is to be done. This will keep the line close to the rod at every point and there will not be loops of slack to become fouled continually in the brush. The thing to aim for in the entire outfit is the elimination of loose ends. The leader should be short and fine, so that the flies may be reeled in close to the rod tip when landing a trout through the brush.

Under normal conditions flies and bait are about equally successful for small brook fishing. While it is

BROOKS, POOLS, STILL-WATERS

a fact that real fly-fishing or rather fly-casting, is precluded by the nature of the stream, still the mountain brook is no place for the duffer with a fly-rod. Indeed, a small stream of this sort requires a deftness, skill, and versatility of expedients in handling rod, line, and flies that is unknown on the larger streams in the open where free casting is the rule. The problem is to get the flies out from twenty to thirty feet without casting in the usual manner, and it is not always an easy one.

Small flies of modest colors are best, such as the coachman, cowdung, Cahill, Beaverkill, and other gray and brown winged flies, and also the various hackles. The smallest sizes should be used, tens and twelves, and even at times the midge flies. More than two flies should never be used, and one is better. As a matter of fact it is seldom that more than one fly can be laid on the water and fished properly, owing to the difficulty of casting and the smallness of the stream, and two flies, also, are just twice as apt to get fouled as one. If two are used they should be attached to the leader quite close together so that both may be fished at the same time in the smallest pools.

The angler will save himself much trouble and annoyance by forgetting to bring a landing net. The use of a net on small trout is at best of questionable propriety or necessity—something like using a ten-gauge on rail—and on the brushy mountain stream it is the most versatile trouble maker you can have along. A very playful little trick of the net fitted with an elastic cord is to catch on a branch, stay behind you to the elastic limit of the cord when you move along, then break loose and snap forward into the small of your back with considerable velocity and no little penetration. The smashing effect, however, is usually upon the net ultimately. Instead of the net carry a little pocket-axe; it is far more useful.

Possibly the greatest factor for success in this sort of fishing is the faculty of going slowly, never hurrying by places which look a little difficult to fish and consequently have probably been neglected by other anglers, and carefully fishing out all fishable water. Here and there, in little clearings and where the stream widens out, you can make short casts in the usual manner; in other places the flies may be got out by simply swinging them over the water as you would cast a "a garden hackle." Often the only way of getting out the flies is to make a "snap cast," using a line about the length of your rod, grasping the end fly between the thumb and forefinger of the left hand, pulling straight back so as to get a good bend in the rod, and then releasing the line—always avoiding the possibility of hooking yourself in the fingers. In this manner very accurate casts may be made after a little practice.

Fishing Methods.

When a trout is hooked, if the banks are so brushy that you cannot beach him or swing—not throw—him out, the fish should be slowly reeled in up to the leader-knot, taking pains not to reel this knot through the tip guide and thus fouling the line, and then brought in through the brush by pulling the rod toward you down low. Many trout will be lost by attempting to land them in this way and it should only be used as a last resort in the worst and most brushy places. Move slowly and quietly, keep as far back from the brook as possible without using too long a line and thus inviting disaster, and use deliberation in the choice of methods for the various little pools, falls, and riffles. The first cast is the one that counts.

When brush fishing a good point to remember is not to strike upward but backward or toward you. If you strike upward a miss always means a hang-up, but if you strike by quickly moving the rod toward you and keeping it low down, this will happen far less frequently. An effective method is to strike not with the rod but by quickly pulling in the line through the guides with the left hand. The two-handed fly-caster who habitually uses the slack-line cast becomes very expert at striking small trout in brushy streams in this manner.

As a general thing you will not often find trout much over a quarter of a pound in the average small mountain stream; but conditions vary and occasionally you will take or see taken trout weighing a pound or more. Many small brooks, although not very wide, may be comparatively deep. Those flowing through meadow lands and with sandy or muddy bottoms are apt to be of this sort; possibly the brook may not be over six feet wide, but there will be many places where the depth is from three to five feet with fine trout shelters hollowed out beneath the banks.

Exceptional Streams.

There is a brook of this sort, well-known to the writer, which flows partly in Connecticut and partly in Massachusetts. Its average width is not over five feet and the stream bed is black mud. Mostly it flows through an alder swamp, with here and there a very little open fishing in old slashings. Anglers who have "sand" enough to fish this brook through the swamp—football is child's play in comparison—show baskets of trout that would drive the average angler crazy. Many times the creels show from a dozen to twenty trout, not a single one less than a pound, and running from that up to two pounds and a half. This is not a fish story alleged but one experienced.

In view of this it is a good plan to find out from local anglers whether the stream you are to fish has a reputation for an occasional large trout and outfit accordingly. It is rather disconcerting, to say the least, when you are sure that a quarter of a pound is the limit for the stream, to have a pound fish roll up to your flies—and a rattled fisherman means a lost fish.

Fishing the Pools and Still-waters

Although fly-casting consists for the most part of fast-water fishing, yet in nearly every stream there are many deep, still pools and often long reaches of still-water wherein are resident the very largest trout of the river. Aristocratic seclusion is theirs, and their rule is absolute. Quietly the activities of the pool go on about them. At times a muskrat or mink stems silently the still surface of the waters. Nervous kingfishers perch momentarily on overhanging branches and then, rattling, seek other vantage points. Insect

The Brook Trout of the Still-waters.

BROOKS, POOLS, STILL-WATERS

life is abundant about the pool, from brilliant butterflies to invisible midges. At times a kindergarten of foolish minnows ventures into the sacred precincts; scattered, with some lost and many wounded, they dart away before the onslaught of the weighty residents. Thus living at ease, with much good eating which comes to them quite independently of effort on their part, serene in the knowledge of their superior strength and size, the brook trout of the still-waters wax ever mightier and, from the angler's viewpoint, more desirable.

Dark-skinned fish, these, from long residence in deep water well shaded, and in shape chunky and full-bellied. Dignified and deliberate of mien are they and of temperament highly suspicious, for the reward of the easy life of the pool is won by those individuals only who are best fitted to survive. Once they too free-lanced in the riffles and rapids with others of their kind, seeking daily sustenance at the risk of divers sudden deaths. In time, however, they assumed formidable proportions and became themselves the lords of the stream. To this distinction they arrived only by exceptionally good fortune and unusual self-protective abilities. It would seem, then, that the angler who would successfully match his skill against the sagacity of these veterans must depend largely upon strategy and the ability to suit tackle to occasion.

In the riffles and rapids no extraordinary skill is needed to lend life-like motion to the flies. Once the cast is made and the flies have alighted upon the water in the desired spot, they are caught by the eddies and

Casting Over Pools. drifted here and there in almost exact imitation of half-drowned, struggling insects. In the still-waters it is different. Here life must be imparted to the flies by skilful handling of rod and line; and, too, more care must be taken in the actual casting, that is, the flies must be dropped upon the water with all possible gentleness. A cast which in all probability would be a successful one in broken water might cause the flies to impact on the glassy surface of the pool with a splash quite sufficient to prevent any hope of a rise in the immediate vicinity.

The primary necessity for a successful cast over quiet water is that it be made gently. Then comes the necessity of so handling the tackle that the line shall not become slack; that the flies shall stay well up on the surface and appear alive; and that immediate advantage may be taken of a strike. Here again working the line with the left hand, stripping it through the guides, solves the problem. In this way the flies are under full control. Also your rod need not be raised much from a line parallel with the water, and when, as sometimes happens, a fish rises when the flies are close to you, the rod is in a position to handle the strike—which is not the case when it is pointing to the exact center of the high heavens.

Striking. As a rule the brook trout of the still-waters strikes slowly, in a manner quite different from the voracious dash of his brothers of the rapids. Leisurely he rises to the surface and sucks in the fly, natural or artificial, and with equal deliberation returns to his lair. It is necessary to strike at the psychological moment. The tendency is to strike too quickly, a better fault than to strike too late. If the rise is missed, it is well not to re-cast immediately, but to rest the pool for a few moments, a matter, by the way, requiring no little self-restraint in case the rising fish is a large one.

Should the pool be a small one it is probable that one trout only is resident. But if the pool is spacious, with many submerged logs and rocks, with shady caves beneath overhanging banks, or other ambushes beloved by trout, it is quite probable that several fish are located there. If you would land more than one of them you must be careful to land that one quietly and with the least possible disturbance. Restrict his play to the limit of tackle safety and beach or net him without noise. If you are successful in this the pool may yield a brace or two of good fish. At times casting from the head of the pool raises no fish, but if you go around and cast from below you will often cause one to change his mind. Every pool is best fished from both above and below.

Playing and Landing.

In the matter of flies the residents of the pool are discriminating in the highest degree. Day and night myriads of insects swarm over the still waters. Grasshoppers and crickets suicide continually from the bank; grubs drop down from the trees; the riffles and rapids deposit a varied menu in the temporary resting place of the pool. As a consequence of this glut of good things the fish are apt to

Flies.

be reluctant in rising and must be skilfully teased. The taking qualities of the sunken and dry-fly should not be forgotten as successful variations of the orthodox method of casting. The dry-fly, although not suitable for fast water, can often be used to advantage when fishing the pool. Also patience and still more patience is necessary when trying conclusions with the wise ones of the quiet water.

Taught in the school of experience the danger of strange insects, in the daytime the residents of the pool are wary when the silk and feathered imitations flutter over the water. But at dusk and in the moonlight this natural shyness seems to depart in some degree and such times are propitious ones for the fly-caster. In a way this seems to be taking an unfair advantage over the fish and, too, the trout do not fight as strongly under these conditions. However, if it is a case of night fishing or bacon for breakfast, the sporting ethics of the matter may properly be disregarded. Although subversive of the general axiom of light flies for dark days and dark ones for light days, it is a fact that in night fishing a soberly colored fly is sometimes more taking than one lighter in coloration. If the white miller fails to attract, try the black gnat.

Night Fishing.

The angler who customarily fishes a stream wherein there are many wide pools likely to harbor large trout should select his outfit with the greatest care, with a view to fishing for the larger trout and allowing the small fry to stay in the water. In other words, the angler should make

Other Tackle.

the big trout the chief object of the day's fishing and not have his tackle suited only to small fish. One reason why the "big one" so often gets away is because trout fishing to many anglers means merely the taking of numerous young fish little better than fingerlings and when a trout of good fighting size takes hold of the tackle he easily tears it apart. Of course, if the chance of striking a really good fish is very remote, as when fishing the smallest streams, it is best to use the very lightest tackle, for therein lies the sport of taking the smaller trout.

Strong tackle, suited to fairly large trout, is far from implying coarse tackle. Coarse tackle in trout fishing is of almost no use save on very exceptional occasions. The brook trout is by nature one of the wariest of game fish and in most localities has in addition a very thorough education in angling affairs. Strong tackle is not necessarily coarse, but to obtain it of a quality good enough to embody both strength and fineness as regards caliber and material it is necessary to use judgment in its selection and to pay the price. It may be noted here, although not enlarged upon, that coarse tackle is not always strong tackle. The distinction between tackle too coarse and that which is suitable, although easily recognized in concrete cases by both fish and fishermen, is difficult to set down in so many words. Frequently it may be a matter of inch-thousandths and the micrometer caliper.

Dry-fly Fishing

It is in connection with pool and still-water fishing that the use of the dry-fly can most appropriately be considered. It is not at all probable that dry-fly fishing will ever reach in this country the popularity it has attained in England; the average of stream conditions is against it. Fishing with the dry-fly is by no means a new thing and a few American anglers have practiced it for a good many years. Recently, however, much greater interest has been taken in the subject than formerly and for that reason it seems best to include here a brief description of the dry-fly caster's methods.

The following notes on dry-fly fishing—which the present writer could not hope to equal in comprehensiveness, clearness, and brevity—were written by Mr. Alfred Herbert, of Kenilworth, England, and published in *Forest and Stream* for June 15, 1907. In the opinion of the writer it is the very best short description of dry-fly methods ever printed, and for that reason I take the liberty of quoting, in part, as follows:

"In this style of fishing we invariably fish up stream, and in our clear waters here we are able to see the trout distinctly. The angler looks out for a fish which is actually rising and feeding on the natural floating insect. This, of course, only happens when there is a rise of flies on the water. On some days there will be very little, if any, rise of insects, and consequently very few fish to be caught; at other times, in favorable weather, rises may be more or less continuous during the day, but the best part of the rise usually concentrates itself into short periods, the best time being generally between eleven and three o'clock in the spring, while later in the year there is often a good evening rise after sundown, if the weather is warm and the atmosphere free from mist.

"When a feeding fish is seen, the angler's object is to get as near to him from below as possible without scaring the fish. This necessitates a good deal of progression after the manner of the serpent, it being essential above all things to keep low. The fly chosen should be as near as possible a reproduction of the natural insect on the water. The line, which is of plaited silk, dressed in linseed oil under the air pump, is carefully greased, preferably with red deer fat, but vaseline or hard mutton suet answers equally well. The object of greasing the line is to insure that it shall float lightly on the surface of the water. If not greased —no matter how well it may be dressed—it soon tends to be waterlogged, and in this condition sinks below the surface of the water when drawn in, dragging the fly with it under the water and thus soaking the latter.

"The line we use here is generally fairly heavy and preferably tapers to a fine point. Only one fly is used in this style of fishing. The fly itself is lightly touched with a spot of odorless paraffin from the small bottle which is carried on one's waistcoat button. After anointing the fly with paraffin, I find it well to absorb the excess paraffin on a dry handkerchief; then by making a few false casts in the air the fly is further dried, and nothing but a minute suspicion of paraffin remains on the fly; otherwise any excess of the paraffin forms a film on the water, which is distinctly and detrimentally visible to the fish.

"Having now got within easy range of the rising fish, the angler's object is to drop the fly about two or three feet above him, so that it shall come down in a natural position, with its wings erect (or 'cocked,' as we call it). It should fall on the water quite lightly, and the least splash of the line is fatal, the fish in these waters apparently having eyes all over as well as in their heads. It is important that the fly should travel at precisely the same pace as other natural flies which are floating freely on the water, otherwise a ripple or drag is set up, and our fish will not look at a fly which has the slightest suspicion of drag.

"Drag is very difficult to overcome under some conditions; it is caused by the stream running faster in some parts than in others; for instance, if one is casting across a river, and the water in the center is running faster than at the side on which the fly falls, the pull of the current on the line tends to draw the fly faster than the water around it, and this sets up 'positive drag.' If, on the other hand, owing to the conformation of the stream, the water is running more rapidly at the side where the fly falls than it is in the center where the line falls, then the line will hold back the fly and set up drag of another kind—'negative drag.'

"If all these various difficulties are overcome, and if the fly happens to appeal to the fish as a suitable morsel, it is taken, often with a great show of confidence. The subsequent proceedings are exciting, but are, of course, quite familiar. . . . The conditions that are most favorable to dry-fly fishing are, first of all, that the surface of the water should be smooth enough to enable the fly to float and to enable the angler to see it; secondly, that the fish be actually feeding, obviously on some floating insect. Under these conditions I believe the dry-fly will kill fish on any river; but of course in rapid streams, where the surface is broken up by rocks and the current is strong, the conditions are undoubtedly entirely against the dry-fly fisherman. . . .

"The great attraction of dry-fly fishing is the actual seeing of the individual fish, the stalking for him, and his ultimate capture; in fact, you see the whole performance and fish consciously for one individual trout, whereas in the wet-fly system (which, of course, is also largely used in England), one casts simply into a likely piece of water and hopes for the best. . . ."

In addition to the above it remains only to be said that to use the dry-fly method it is not absolutely imperative to cast to a visibly rising fish, for if he chooses the angler may fish all the water as in wet-fly fishing. It should also be noted that while the majority of dry-flies used in England are close imitations of the insect life of the streams other flies which are sometimes used successfully are not exact imitations but rather of the sort known as "fancy."

CHAPTER IV

FLY-CASTING AND FLY-FISHING

IT is quite possible for an angler to take a good many brook trout without being an expert fly-caster. Mere mechanical proficiency in casting is by no means the most important factor in resultful fly-fishing. A good many other things, such as knowledge of trout haunts and habits and what is fishable water, have weight in deciding the success or non-success of the angler's day on the stream.

But notwithstanding the fact that fly-casting is not all of fly-fishing, it is very well for the angler to be able to cast better than the other fellow; given two anglers of equal stream experience and like knowledge of brook trout characteristics, the better caster will assuredly make the better showing. The very poor caster, too, no matter how wise he may be in general angling affairs, will certainly offset his superior theoretical knowledge by his awkwardness in practical fishing. Also, apart from the application of fly-casting to fly-fishing, it is a fact that mere fly-casting is good sport—witness the popularity of tournament casting. The man who has acquired some expertness in casting the fly gets a great deal of pleasure from this alone.

Most of the written treatises in books and magazines on how to cast with the fly-rod, while as a whole correct, fail somewhat in their purpose because the authors, in treating the entire subject of rod handling, do not place sufficient emphasis on certain particular phases of the matter. Good fly-casting is dependent upon close attention to a number of individual details, some more important than others, but each of such importance that if any one of them is neglected the results are not of the best. With long practice observance of these details becomes automatic, but the beginner must keep them firmly fixed in his mind. The following is not an attempt to teach fly-casting, but merely to emphasize certain details which, at first glance, may have seemed inconsiderable and consequently may not have been strictly observed.

How to Improve Your Fly-casting

In the first place let us consider the apparently unimportant question of how to hold the rod, i.e., the position of the rod hand on the handgrasp. Nine out of ten beginners at fly-casting would say immediately that, provided the caster does not drop the rod, the method of holding is immaterial. Now the veteran fly-caster and the books on fly-fishing will tell you that the proper way to hold the rod is to have the thumb of the rod hand extended along the upper surface of the handgrasp and not bent around it. There must be some reason for this opinion and advice of the experts, and there is a very good one. In fact, there are two reasons.

Good fly-casting, whether considered from the standpoint of accuracy, delicacy, or distance, depends on getting your wrist into the cast. If you make it a practice to grasp the rod as above indicated, with the thumb lying straight along the top of the handgrasp, you will soon find that you are getting your wrist into the cast to a much greater extent than ever before. And when you once find out what a great difference this makes, you will know why, perhaps, your casting theretofore has not been eminently satisfactory or proficient.

If you cast practically at arm's length, as you will often see done, delivering the line with a sweeping motion of the entire arm from the shoulder, **Straight-arm Casting.** of what use to you is a finely constructed fly-rod, made especially with a view to the utmost speed and resilience? Straight-arm casting fails entirely in putting the rod itself to work; the arm motion does it all—and very poorly. But once get the wrist into the cast and you will find the rod, if it is a good one, bending from handgrasp to tip-end and, as a result, the line jumping away as if sent for.

Again, this method of holding the rod results in a greater ability to cast accurately. The rod is under perfect control and the direction of the **An Aid to Accuracy.** cast, under favorable conditions, will deviate very slightly from the point aimed for. Target shooting with a rifle and casting with a fly-rod are similar in that both, quite naturally, require aim. With the thumb pointing along the handgrasp proper initial aim is instinctive and the rod is guided in the right direction throughout the cast.

FLY-CASTING AND FLY-FISHING

Another very important point is not to carry the rod too far back on the back cast. This fault simply means that too long a time will elapse between the forward and back casts and that the line will become dead in the rear of the caster. On the back cast the rod should go but slightly beyond the perpendicular; this will keep the line high in the air—the object to be attained—where it will respond at once to a correctly timed forward cast. The line must be kept alive throughout the period covered by the forward and back casts, and nothing is more apt to kill a cast than letting the rod go too far back. You will occasionally see fly-casters carry the rod so far to the rear that the line actually falls on the water behind them.

The Back Cast.

Try to get a high back cast. When the tip of the rod, in the arc described by the rod in the back cast, reaches a point just over your head, stop the rod; the momentum and bend of the rod will then carry it to just about the right position for starting the forward cast.

And now about starting the forward and back casts: the chief mistake made by beginners in starting the back cast is in starting it too easily. When ready lift the line from the water with a strong, snappy, backward wrist motion, so that it will have sufficient speed to straighten out behind you before beginning to fall toward the water. This, too, will help in attaining the high back cast mentioned above. Do not delay starting the back

Timing the Casts.

cast too long; begin it when the flies are well away from you.

In the paragraph above I have suggested waiting for the line to straighten out behind the caster on the back cast, that is, before beginning the forward cast. Instantaneous photographs of expert casters, however, show that in actual practice the line does not entirely straighten out in the rear before the forward cast is started; that, in fact, there is a considerable loop at the end of the line which straightens out just after the caster begins the forward cast. The theory of this is quite plain. If, when casting a rather long line, you wait until the line becomes quite straight behind you, you wait just long enough for the line to lose its life. The forward cast, then, should be started when the line, having passed to the rear of the caster, first begins to pull appreciably on the rod.

On the other hand, do not start the forward cast too quickly, because this is liable to snap off the end fly. Correct timing of the forward cast is one of the greatest factors in clean-cut casting. Do not start the forward cast too strenuously. The speed of the rod when passing through the arc of the forward cast should be greater toward the finish. At the end of the forward cast the rod should be a little above parallel with the water.

In the matter of rod handling, then, the chief points for the fly-caster to observe, as regards primarily the overhead cast, are these: To hold the rod with the thumb extended along the upper surface of the handgrasp; not to carry the rod too far back on the back

FLY-CASTING AND FLY-FISHING

cast; not to delay the back cast too long, and to start it forcefully; to start the forward cast when the line first begins to pull on the rod, and to start it rather easily and finish strongly; and, finally, not to allow the rod to go too far down toward the water at the end of the forward cast.

We come now to a very important factor in good fly-casting, one which, it seems to the writer, is never sufficiently emphasized—indeed, is usually entirely disregarded—in the written treatises on fly-casting. I refer to the matter and manner of using the left hand, taking it for granted that the caster is right-handed, to manipulate the line; the reader will please consider everything said in reference thereto as written in capitals.

Two-handed Casting.

Briefly, the caster should grasp the line with his left hand, between the reel and the first guide, and all paying out and retrieving of the line, either when casting, fishing the flies, or playing a trout, should be with the left hand. The advantages of this method of line handling are manifold, and ability to perform it skilfully is of the utmost importance. A loop of line of reasonable length, not so long as to invite fouling, should always be maintained between the reel and the first guide so that at the end of the forward cast (when the hold of the left hand on the line is slightly relaxed) this loop will shoot out through the rod guides, thereby adding a number of feet to the cast. Casting at any thing over moderate distances can only be done by this method.

Learning to use the left hand in the above manner

when casting is one of the most difficult things in fly-casting, particularly if you have become accustomed to one-handed casting, but it is certainly worth the trouble of acquiring it; in fact, its advantages and applications in various directions both in casting and fishing the flies are so numerous that they can merely be suggested at this point. Particular reference is made elsewhere to certain situations wherein the two-handed fly-caster has every advantage over the caster whose education has not progressed thus far. In the writer's opinion and, it may safely be said, in the opinion of every man who has done much fly-fishing, the one thing above all others is to learn how to handle the line with your left hand.

Following the above suggestions should certainly result in adding a number of feet to your average casting without any determined effort to gain distance. In fact the gaining of distance by mere muscle should be studiously avoided if for no other reason than that very long casting is usually very poor fishing, except, of course, where reaching out is absolutely necessary on account of natural conditions. The chronic distance caster generally overcasts his water, neglecting good water nearby for the sake of seeing his flies come down far-off. There is a certain satisfaction in this without doubt, but it is not good fly-fishing. Strenuous effort is not at all necessary for reasonable distance fishing casts; tournament casting is another thing. If you can succeed in getting the true science of casting down to a fine point, the harmonious action of wrist, rod, and line, everything

Distance vs. Accuracy.

FLY-CASTING AND FLY-FISHING 63

done just right and at just the right time, it will surprise you how easily the flies may be sent for comparatively long distances. Accuracy is the thing to strive for.

The overhead cast is the foundation of all fly-casting: other casts, such as the wind cast and the side cast, being merely variations to meet weather conditions or the natural formation of the stream. As a matter of fact, the wind and side casts, employed against the wind or when the danger of hanging-up precludes the overhead cast, are used quite as much as the overhead, especially the side cast which is a very efficient and practical fishing method. This latter cast, too, it is claimed, is the one best adapted to laying down a dry-fly cocked and dry upon the water, and is recommended to the dry-fly caster above all others. The fly-caster who is reasonably proficient with the overhead cast can pick up the wind and side casts very easily.

Other Casts.

The wind cast is decidedly not a pretty one, but in a strong wind, blowing directly toward the caster, it is the only method which will get out the flies any reasonable distance. Much accuracy under the conditions is not practicable, and any degree of delicacy in dropping the flies impossible and unnecessary, for the ruffled surface of the water hides any fault in this direction.

The Wind Cast.

The back cast is made in the usual manner—the wind cast is an overhead cast—but the forward cast is a strong downward chopping motion, moving the rod hand outward and downward, with a quick, strong snap of the wrist, and the rod should come down closer to the water than in the usual overhead cast. The wind cast will put out the line a fair fishing distance under very adverse conditions, but it is tiring and particularly hard on a light fly-rod. However, it is well worth knowing. It sometimes happens that trout will be found rising very freely on a windy, blustering day, even when they have shown no interest in the artificials under presumably more favorable conditions. Using this cast you will have fair success when the other fellow is climbing trees after his flies or sitting behind a fence waiting for the wind to go down—and the wind never goes down.

In the side cast the rod travels back in the back cast parallel with the water and not far above the waist-line; the rod hand must be kept down low with the back of the hand toward the water. The line should be thrown backward traveling three or four feet above the surface of the stream, and the forward cast must be started quickly and timed correctly, since the line has only a little distance to fall before striking the water. The latter contingency should be avoided for several reasons, and of these not the least important is that you are liable to rise a trout when the flies strike behind you— a very disconcerting situation and one liable to result in a smash-up. I have seen this happen several times.

The Side Cast.

The side cast should always be used where overhanging branches invite a hang-up even when by taking chances and using the overhead cast you might gain greater distance. Under such conditions it is better to move up slowly and quietly, or, if necessary, get out of the stream and still-hunt your trout from the bank. A hang-up with the consequent maneuvers to get free always spoils sport in the immediate vicinity.

How to Fish the Flies

The one thing which definitely distinguishes the fly-fishing beginner from the fly-fishing veteran is the manner in which the cast of flies is handled. If, with some fly-fishing experience to make your judgment competent, you follow the veteran fly-caster as he wades down the stream, you will see that always the flies alight where they will do the most good, that the manner of handling the cast varies with the water and other conditions, that the cast passes over every bit of likely water, and that always the flies are fished with malice aforethought and with little or nothing of the chuck-and-chance-it about the process.

But if you choose to share as a spectator—quite the best way—the varied fortunes and misfortunes of the fly-casting novice on the stream, you will see another sort of fishing. Everything is haphazard and without definite plan; good water and poor are fished out with equal futility; in fact, the novice, provided he can get the flies out on the water, somehow, anyhow, or anywhere, and again retrieve them, is satisfied that he is fly-fishing and damns the stream as trout deserted when, in consequence of his methods, or rather, lack of method, the results are nil. To put it in another way: The manner in which the flies are fished distinguishes the fly-fisherman from the mere fly-caster, whether or no the fly-caster, as such, be expert or otherwise.

As in selecting a fly-rod one is rather more apt to consider primarily its casting qualities than its suitability to playing and landing trout, so is one prone when speaking of fly-fishing to consider rather the act of casting the flies than the ways of fishing them. As a matter of practical angling, however, one of the chief functions of the fly-rod is the playing and landing of trout; and casting the fly, apart from tournament work, is a mere mechanical preliminary to fishing the flies. Fly-fishing begins when the flies are on the water. Ability to cast well cannot be over-rated, but fishing the flies is even more important.

To fish the flies properly one must know what is fishable water—"where the trout hide"—after which correct manipulation of the flies is the important factor. The stream localities especially favored by the trout vary considerably as regards their natural characteristics with different streams and, also, with the different species of trout—brook, brown, or rainbow. Also the time of year, as noted in the preceding chapter, whether early or late in the season, determines to quite an extent where the most trout will be found. Knowledge of brook trout habits and an acquaintance with the stream gained by whipping it a good many times will show the angler which is the fishable water in any given stream.

Fishable Water.

The manner in which to handle the cast of flies is, however, more or less a matter of conjecture, immediate results from various ways of fishing the cast determining

FLY-CASTING AND FLY-FISHING 67

very often for the time being the manner most effective. It is a fact that the angler who becomes wedded to one way and sticks to that way through thick and thin, no matter what the time of year, condition of water, or character of the stream, will catch trout, but the angler who chooses to be versatile in his methods will catch more.

Versatility in Fly-fishing.

Books on fly-fishing usually dismiss the subject of how to fish the flies with the brief and apparently satisfactory advice: Imitate as closely as possible the actions of the natural insect. Of course, imitation of the natural insect is the thing to strive for, but—just how do you go about it? The result of this advice is that the novice, with the very best intentions, generally skips, twitches, and flutters the flies about on the water, sometimes making them skip gaily up-stream against a sixty-mile current, all in the fond belief that he is imitating nature to the limit. In the opinion of the writer, founded upon a fair success in trout fly-fishing due probably more than anything else to avoiding this sort of nature fake, no worse way of handling the cast can possibly be employed.

Imitation of Nature.

Do not skip the flies about over the water. Exact imitation of nature in trout fly-fishing is most closely approached by dry-fly methods; and twitching and fluttering the flies forms no part of the science of dry-fly fishing. By all means, eschew dragging the flies up-stream against sixty-mile currents because, as a matter of fact, the natural insect would, of course, be going the other way at "current rates."

In the opinion of experienced fly-casters the most successful method of casting and fishing the flies is at right angles to the stream, cross-current, allowing the flies to sweep along downstream with the current over the desirable places, always taking pains to have a fairly taut line. Usually the slightly submerged fly is the most effective. This method it would seem is, in a way, a compromise between the up-stream and down-stream methods.

The Cross-Current Cast.

The caster who uses this method should employ the slack-line cast, described above in this chapter, drawing in the line gradually through the rod guides with the left hand as the flies work around and down-stream in order to maintain a taut line. The course traveled by the flies is practically a quarter-circle from a point in front of the caster to one directly below him and downstream. They are then lifted and another cast made from a stand lower down. Care should be taken that the leader and flies float fairly straight, that is, the leader should not be bent so that the end fly tails along too far behind the dropper. A taut line, watching the effect of the current and holding the rod pretty well up, will obviate this.

The extent to which the flies should be submerged varies with the weather and water conditions, and also with the temporary likes and dislikes of the trout. On a slightly flooded and discolored stream, or early in the season, or on a very windy day, or in very rough, broken water, the chances are that the considerably submerged

The Submerged Fly.

fly will be the most effective. Fishing in this manner, when the flies get well away from you, you will possibly not see the rising trout but must strike by the "feel"; it is very difficult and a matter of much practice to hook a fish under these circumstances. Often you will not know that the trout has struck and when you lift the flies for the back cast you will merely prick him and roll him over in the water. It goes without saying that the feelings of both parties to this transaction are considerably hurt.

But with practice and the employment of constant vigilance it becomes possible for the angler to hook his fish "sight unseen" with fair regularity. **Striking Un-** In fact, the fly-caster develops a sort of **seen Trout.** second-sight which tells him when to strike even when occasionally he has not felt the fish or even seen the flash of the trout in the water. As a general thing fewer strikes will be missed if they come when the cast is carrying around and down-stream and before the line straightens out below the angler. It is always well to re-cast immediately as soon as the line straightens out directly down-stream and not to allow the flies to play around in the swift current at the end of a taut line. A trout striking under these conditions is seldom hooked securely, and the force of the water helps him to tear away before you can get things into proper shape to play with him. Fishing a deeply submerged fly is not very desirable from a sporting point of view and the method should only be employed as a last resort, when it is often very effective.

Under normal conditions, with clear and fairly

smooth water and on calm days, the flies should be only slightly submerged—in fact, should be fished quite on the surface, sinking only to the extent caused by their weight.

The Surface Fly.

This may be attained by always keeping the point of the rod well up and taking care to strip in the line with the proper rapidity. If the line becomes too slack or the rod point drops too low the flies will become drowned at once. They should as far as possible be allowed to follow the natural trend of the current, just as a derelict insect would float, following through the eddies and whirls without noticeable restraint from the line. You may be sure that trout know where to lie in the stream in order to intercept insects floating down with the current; and that if your flies follow the natural course of the current in a natural manner, they will pass over the majority of the best "lies" in a way calculated to produce results.

A very foxy cast is to drop your flies on a patch of floating foam. Do not immediately drag the flies through the foam but allow them to lie upon and float with it, exactly as the natural insect caught in this manner would do, finally sinking through. Foam patches collect numbers of insects and the trout know this.

A Foxy Cast.

The method of casting above described, at right angles to the current, is the one to tie to; it is the best way to fish the flies under almost all conditions. But, of course, there are times and places when and where this method is impracticable. Often it is impossible to reach a

Pool Fishing.

proper stand from which to cast cross-current; and, too, the method naturally requires a current to carry the flies. This last precludes the use of the cross-current cast over pools and still-waters.

In places of this sort it is necessary to impart natural action to the flies by manipulation of the rod and line, but anything in the nature of fussiness or too obvious motion should be avoided. The cast should be made lightly and the flies allowed to remain for a moment where they alight and then withdrawn a little and quietly. Over pools and still-waters it is best not to allow them to remain in one spot too long; that is, they should not be dragged any considerable distance from the point where they first fell. It is better to cast frequently, relying upon repeated casts to cover the pool thoroughly.

A very important thing is to be careful always about the first cast you make over any likely spot. The tendency, even with experienced fly-casters who know better, is to make this first cast rather carelessly and as a sort of experiment. Consequently a good fish is often raised and lost on account of the angler's not being ready for him. As a general thing—every fly-fishing rule has its numerous exceptions—a trout that is in a rising mood will come for the first or second cast, and it is rather more apt to come for the first than the second. In view of this always make the first cast over any new place fully prepared for trouble. If the trout rises when you are only at half-attention and is missed, or is pricked and lost, the chances are numerous that you have seen

The First Cast.

the last of him—a pricked trout never comes to the fly again.

Another thing—before you cast over any difficult place where the current is very swift, or the banks rocky and steep, or the water too deep to wade, always look over the situation and make up your mind just where is the best place to land a fish under the circumstances and how one may best be handled; then pick your place to cast from accordingly. Then when you strike a good-sized trout you will not be rattled about what to do next but will be ready to go right after him. If you are unprepared and merely hang on to the fish while you are trying to decide what to do with him the chances are that he will tear away or foul you before you can make up your mind. Often you will see anglers casting from places where it would be simply impossible for them to save a trout if one were hooked.

CHAPTER V

THE BAIT-CASTER AND THE SWEET-WATER BASSES

SOME years ago Dr. James A. Henshall, whose name is so intimately and favorably connected with the sporting and natural history of the sweet-water basses, stated that the black bass—"inch for inch and pound for pound the gamest fish that swims"—would eventually become the leading game fish of America. It may be safely said that at the present time the truth of this statement is quite evident. Fly-fishing for trout and casting for bass, barring stream fishing with flies where the two methods are closely approximate, are very different propositions; but comparisons are always -odious and we will not here argue the case of the Brook Trout *vs.* the Black Bass. It is probably a fact that an impartial jury of anglers impaneled from the country at large would bring in a verdict in favor of the defendant—the black bass. An enthusiastic bass fisherman, whom the writer met one day at his camp on the shore of a little lake in the Berkshires, summed up the matter to the satisfaction of

Bait-casting in General.

all present in this way: "I like to fish for brook trout," he said, "but I prefer to catch black bass."

More than anything else the introduction of the short bait-casting rod and the general taking up by anglers of casting from the free-running reel has served to popularize the black bass and bass fishing. Bait-casting from the reel is an inherently interesting angling method and in time will supersede among anglers any other form or forms of bass fishing. At the present time the method, while in very general use, cannot be said to be universal in any such degree as fly-casting for trout is generally practiced. But that it will eventually become the generally accepted and universally accredited form of sportsmanlike bass fishing now seems a certainty.

The Natural History of the Black Bass

You must know something of the habits of the black bass to fish for him successfully, and this is particularly true in the case of the devotee of bait-casting. Given a lake or stream with bass therein, something more is necessary than merely getting into a boat or a pair of waders, selecting some spot that looks sufficiently wet, and then casting for "general results." The small and large-mouth bass spawn during the months of May and June, the exact time depending upon the temperature. In water of a comparatively high temperature the spawning period is prior to that in waters lower in temperature, and in rivers the bass spawn earlier than in lakes and ponds. The nest is guarded by the male fish, and for some time after the eggs have hatched the

BAIT-CASTER AND BASSES

male parent guards the young fish. Small-mouths choose a gravelly bottom for building the nest, but the large-mouths sometimes do not discriminate in this regard. The spawning takes place in the shallows, and for some time thereafter, during the first days of the open season, the bass remain in moderately shallow water. At this time the bait-caster should fish on the surface.

When lake-fishing, parallel the shore in your boat or canoe, casting shoreward to the edge of the weeds, in **Early Fishing.** the shade of overhanging rocks, about lily-pads and submerged trees and places of like nature. Find out where the bars are in the lake you are fishing and cast in to the edge of these. If the bar is a large one, forming an expansive shallow place, perhaps, as often occurs, well out in the middle of the lake, fish the whole of it. If you are fishing waters new to you, get some local angler or guide to locate the various bars. Once located you should take their bearings very carefully so that you can find them again. Looking for a lost bar in a big lake is an almost hopeless undertaking.

Thus early in the season the water will be fairly clear of weeds and the angler can cast close in-shore without fouling the tackle. In quiet bays where there are lily-pads and flags, and the bottom has a tendency to be muddy, you will find the large-mouths. Off sandy bars and where gravel bottom predominates, or where the bottom is rocky, you may expect to find the small-mouth bass. The two often co-exist in the same pond or lake, and when caught you can easily differentiate them by observing the relative position of the angle of the jaw and the eye. In the large-mouth the angle of the jaw is perceptibly to the rear of the eye; in the small-mouth it is exactly underneath.

As the season advances the bass work out into deeper and cooler water. Now, except early or late in the day, when the fish may be feeding in the shallows, the bait-caster should use an under-water bait. Locate the spring-holes, for at this time the bass, particularly the small-mouths, congregate about these; if there are shady places along-shore, where the water is of fair depth, try your luck there. For much success at this season you must go down to the fish. If you find the bait you are using is not successful put on lead and the chances are it will make a difference. An ordinary spoon is a good lure for this purpose. When leaded it sinks rapidly and if not reeled in too quickly, travels at a good depth. A small dipsey sinker is the best to use.

Summer Fishing.

It is a mistake to rely wholly, as do some bait-casters, upon some form of surface bait. There are times, when, as every fly-fisherman has reason to know, trout and bass are not in a rising mood. As your boat moves along the shore you should whip the places which appear promising very thoroughly. One or two casts are sufficient for any one spot, but the next cast should not be more than three or four feet away. Sometimes a bass will only strike the bait when it is cast very close to him. This is particularly the case when the fish are lying close in-shore among the weeds and rushes.

During September and October the water is gradually cooling and the bass are again to be found to quite an extent in the shallows. Most of the summer weed growths are dying down, the clouding effect of the summer "working" has passed away, and the water is now pure and clear. All things considered, this is the best time for bass fishing, especially for the bait-caster. New life seems to have been imparted to the bass and they will rise freely and strike the bait with emphasis. At this time, during the early fall, surface fishing is generally very successful and the admirer of the floating bait for bass may safely give his preference full rein.

Autumn Fishing.

For stream fishing the above methods should be modified to suit the occasion. Wade wherever possible or, if the stream is too deep for this, use a canoe—the only craft for river work. In streams small-mouths "use" about the edges of rifts and rapids and in the pools at the foot of rapids; they are fond of lying in the lee of sunken logs where there is a gentle current and underneath shelving banks; you will often find them lying close to the banks underneath overhanging trees or brush and among submerged tree-roots from which the river has fretted the soil away. If there are large-mouths in the stream cast in the quiet coves where there are lily-pads and rushes and in the still, weedy reaches of the river.

River Fishing.

During the middle of the day, unless it is cloudy and dark, casting for bass is usually love's labor lost; even on cloudy days, when conditions appear most favorable, fishing at this time is apt to be unsuccessful. However,

Weather Conditions. when the weather is unseasonably cold, the mid-day fishing is sometimes the best. The early morning hours are the most fruitful in almost all waters, and the late afternoon and evening fishing is, other things being equal, always good. Under normal conditions bass feed principally early and late in the day. In the summer time, however, during the full moon, when the nights are still and almost day-bright, the bass feed during the night, and day-time fishing is usually very poor.

For a good fishing day it is by no means essential that the sky be overcast. A gray day is a good fishing day undoubtedly, but, in the writer's opinion, a bright, snappy day, with a good ripple on the water, is quite as likely to yield results. A bright, still day in the summer time, when the weather is hot, is no fishing day for the bait-caster. Deep-trolling with live bait is about the only practicable method under such conditions. After the long continuance of a certain sort of weather, either bright or dark, dry or rainy, the fishing often falls off and then any change is one for the better.

Minor weather changes are not liable to affect the river bass fishing greatly. Running water, the varying conformation of the banks and stream bottom, the fact that due to the many turns and bends of the river the wind affects in a different way different portions of the stream, these and other factors combine to keep the fishing fairly good under nearly all conditions. The stream bass angler, however, has to pay for his immunity from certain nuisances affecting the lake fisherman in the susceptibility of the stream to sudden rises caused either by local rains or rains nearer the headwaters. When the rise is on and before the water has become too high and discolored is a propitious time; it is, however, something in the nature of a psychological moment, for although the fishing may be very good while it lasts, it lasts but a short time. Then it is a case of waiting for the stream to go down.

The black bass, either the large- or small-mouth, is one of the most erratic of game fishes. Bass fishermen of long experience generally come to the conclusion that, no matter how well acquainted one may be with the waters fished and the customary habits and habitats of the bass therein, it is impossible for one to forecast with any certainty where the bass may be found or what sort of food or bait they may at any time prefer. In general bass habits are in great measure a matter of locality. Not only will a bass taken from a certain lake differ appreciably in coloration, and sometimes slightly in formation, from one taken from a lake closely adjacent, but in the contrasted waters the habits of the fish will differ considerably. As above suggested you cannot do better, when about to fish new waters, than to rely upon the guidance of a resident angler. It is possible that you may know more about bass fishing than he does, but he will know more about the bass in that particular lake than do you.

Bass Habits a Matter of Locality.

The Tackle for Bait-casting

First-class sport in angling for any game fish is essentially a matter of the tackle and methods employed.

As noted above the present great and increasing interest in the black bass and in fishing for him may be attributed largely to the introduction and very general adoption of the short bait-casting rod. Fly-fishing for black bass, since by far the greater part of bass angling is done in lakes—and lake fly-fishing for bass is not apt to be very productive—is difficult to find of a quality good enough to hold the angler's interest permanently. Where good fly-fishing for bass in running water may be had, that method would properly be preferred to bait-casting by the expert with the fly-rod. Barring this, bait-casting with the short casting rod and free-running reel is the most intrinsically interesting of all bass fishing methods and one calculated to afford reasonable sport under almost all conditions.

The writer has elsewhere discussed bait-casting tackle at some length ("Fishing Kits and Equipment"), but in view of the fact that the required tackle and the correct way of casting with it are not nearly as well understood among anglers in general as the tackle and methods for fly-casting, it seems best to include here a few notes on the casting rod, the casting reel and other bait-casting equipment, together with suggestions in regard to the use of the rod in casting.

The typical modern short casting rod, as distinguished from the old style and longer casting rods of which the well-known "Henshall" rod may be taken as an example, and which the short rods have largely superseded, varies in length for practical fishing purposes from five and a half to six feet. For distance

The Bait-casting Rod.

tournament casting, shorter rods are sometimes used. The essential difference in the use of the short rod and that of the long is that the short rod is employed almost exclusively to cast artificial baits, spoons, singlehook fly-spoons, artificial minnows, and pork-rind baits of various descriptions, and to cast them largely with the overhead cast; while the longer rod is best adapted for the live minnow with the side cast. Overhead casting is not practicable with rods much over six feet in length. When fishing it is very advantageous to be able to employ the overhead and side casts at will; also, at the present time, the tendency among bait-casters is very strongly toward the use of artificial baits.

When selecting the bait-casting rod the angler should consider, in addition to the casting qualities of the rod, its suitability to playing and landing fish. Within reason the shorter rods are better suited to long casting, say the rod of five to five and a half feet. But the caster who employs a rod of this length, surely sacrifices efficiency in handling his fish. As a general rule the longer the rod the more control you have over a hooked fish, also the more certain you are of hooking a rising fish. But to still retain good casting qualities in the rod and the ability to use it for both styles of casting, side and overhead, the rod must not be much over six feet; all things considered, the six-foot rod is the best for all general bait-casting purposes. Its material should, for light fishing, be split-bamboo. For heavy fishing in weedy lakes and deep, swift rivers a sturdy rod of bethabara or greenheart is more serviceable.

The guides of the rod must allow free-running of

the line with the least possible friction and for this reason should be fairly large. German silver trumpet guides are very good ones for the purpose, and to increase the ease of casting and lessen line-wear from friction it is well to have agate hand and tip guides, since it is at these points that the most friction occurs. The very best way to fit the rod in the matter of guides is to use narrow raised agates throughout, although this is rather expensive. The reel-seat must, of course, be above the handgrasp, and all rod mountings should preferably be of German silver.

Bait-casting can be done only with a quadruple multiplying reel. It should be rather long in the barrel as compared with the diameter of the side plates. The size may be either eighty or one hundred yards. A very good one—a cheap casting reel is impossible—may be had for seven dollars and upwards. **The Casting Reel and Line.** The position of the reel on the rod is on top of the rod with the handle to the right, and the rod is never to be turned so that the reel is underneath.

As for the line it must be of undressed silk, no waterproofing or enameling; it must also be of small caliber, size G being the most used. No line save an undressed one of small size can be used for casting from the reel.

As noted above the present tendency of anglers in the matter of baits for bass is to use artificial ones almost entirely. **Artificial Baits.** There are a great many of these baits on the market, but only a few of them are either practical or sportsmanlike. The beginner at bait-casting will do well to use one of the floating baits; when he gets into trouble with the reel, as he most assuredly will, the bait will not go to the bottom with the probability of getting fast when the angler is picking out the tangle. The floating baits induce a great many strikes. Personally I use a small bucktail spoon a great deal, and the small spinners fitted with single-hook bass flies are very satisfactory; with these last a quarter-ounce dipsey sinker should be used. Pork-rind baits are usually very successful and these the angler may cut himself or they may be had in preserved form from the tackle dealers. The pork-rind bait is best used on a small white enameled spoon. The various artificial minnows are much used and very successful lures for bait-casting.

Casting from the Reel

There are two methods of casting from the reel, the side cast and the overhead cast. The side cast is the easier one to negotiate and the beginner will do well at first to confine his attention to this. First, the bait, spoon or artificial minnow, is reeled up to within about six inches of the tip guide. The rod, then, pointing appreciably downward below the waistline, is swung at arm's length to the rear of the caster and then brought forward with a steady sweeping motion. Up to the point when the line is to be released and allowed to run out through the guides as a result of the momentum of the swinging rod, the thumb of the rod hand is kept firmly clamped on the line wound on the reel-spool. When the swing of the rod has reached a point where the line when released will shoot out in the desired direction for the cast, the pressure of the thumb on the reel is slightly, not entirely, released; while the line is running out the thumb is constantly pressed very gently on the revolving reel-spool, as otherwise the reel will revolve faster than the line pays out through the guides and a backlash will result.

The whole philosophy of the thing is in educating the thumb to regulate the reel speed and out-running of the line. Finally, when the cast has been made and the line is being reeled in, care must be taken to wind it evenly on the reel. Of course, at the end of the cast when the bait reaches the water the rod is shifted from the right hand to the left so that the right hand may be used on the reel handle. So, for winding the line evenly on the reel spool in the retrieve, guide it with the thumb of the left hand, grasping the rod above the reel with that hand. Casts of from sixty to eighty feet are quite sufficient for good fishing.

In the overhead cast the rod is brought directly back over the shoulder, taking care not to allow it to go too far down behind, and then swung quickly forward. Otherwise the principles are the same as for the side cast. The overhead cast should be started rather slowly, increasing in force, and the line released when the rod tip is about over the caster's head. The rod should be so held that when the line is running out the side plates of the reel are parallel with the water, with the handle-bar on top.

Some Practical Suggestions

When bait-casting for bass with an artificial bait, unless you reel in so quickly that the line is practically taut, the fish must be struck much as in fly-fishing. It sometimes happens, of course, that the bass will strike hard enough to hook himself even on a slack line, but more often the opposite is the case. The strike in bait-casting is one of the things which must be learned when taking up this method of fishing. Primarily it differs from the strike in fly-fishing in that it is made with the left hand, that is, if the caster is right-handed. The education of the left hand to this work is a matter of much practice and naturally the length of time taken to learn it depends upon the skill of the angler in getting the fish to strike as well as upon the natural adaptability of the angler to learning new methods of tackle handling. It is quite possible for an angler to be an expert fly-caster and still be unable to educate his thumb to bait-casting.

When casting toward a fixed point where a bass may be located, such as a patch of lily pads or rushes, or the edge of a bar, the strike of the bass may be expected at the instant the bait strikes the water. For this reason the angler should be careful to start the retrieve at once. When a bass strikes in this manner he usually hooks himself if the line is at all taut. Sometimes a bass will see the bait when it is still moving through the air and will follow its course to the point of contact with the water, when he will strike it. But even under these circumstances it is best to set the hook in the fish, although the strike need not be strenuous.

In the writer's experience more bass are raised and hooked at the moment the lure strikes the water, or almost immediately thereafter, than when the bait is being reeled or trolled in. Certainly a good bait-caster can kill more bass by casting any certain artificial bait than the fisherman who trolls the same bait. It is the motion and impact of the bait upon the water which arouses the fighting blood of the bass and causes him to rise and strike.

Bass as a rule strike an artificial lure from the rear. Of course, when the bait is cast to one side of the fish, he takes advantage of the fact that the shortest distance between two points is a straight line and strikes from the side. But when the bait is being reeled in a bass most often comes to it from the rear. It is for this reason that moderately slow reeling is always most successful. If the lure is moving at too great speed short rises are apt to occur, and if the bass is slightly pricked it is not at all probable that he will come again. Pickerel, it should be noted, almost invariably strike from the side, and here again slow reeling is of importance, for a clean miss frequently results when the bait is moving too fast.

When a bass is fastened at the end of a long cast the tendency of the angler is to hurry him in to the boat, where he can be played to more advantage. This often results in the loss of the fish. It should be remembered that a quadruple multiplying reel is of lightning speed, and consequently fast cranking is not only unnecessary but risky. When fishing in very weedy waters, however, it is often a case of speedy reeling or the loss of the fish in the weeds. Here the situation offers only a choice of evils, and the balance of advantage is probably on the side of fast reeling. A bass can imbed himself in a mass of weeds in an unappreciable moment, and you will then often lose not only fish but tackle. As a general rule, however, avoid trying to lead a big fish until he shows an inclination for being led.

It sometimes happens, although rarely, that a bass will follow the bait until it is almost up to the boat before he strikes it. This is a situation productive of several different kinds of disasters, unless the angler keeps his wits about him. If the rod is perpendicular, or nearly so, at the moment the bass strikes, a smashed tip is liable to result if any attempt is made to set the hook. The chances are that the bass has hooked himself and he should be slacked instead of struck and only slightly restrained until he is in a position where he can be played advantageously.

Naturally it is impossible to state any invariable rule as to how, when, or where a bass will strike. Individual fish act differently under like circumstances and bass in different waters vary much in habits. As in trout fly-fishing it is the often unexpected manner in which the bass makes known his presence that affords one of the principal attractions of the sport.

When the Bloom is Off the Water

Other things being equal, the question of when to go is quite as important to the sportsman, especially the angler, as the question of where to go. No matter how well the sportsman may be outfitted in the matter of tackle and experience and how wisely and well he may have chosen the locality for the sport he desires, if the question of the proper time to go, the season of the year in its relation to the habits of the game, is not duly considered the trip may result in absolute failure. This is particularly true as regards selecting the time for a bass fishing trip.

In most States the open season for black bass is a very long one, much longer than for brook trout. As a general thing the law protects the bass only during the spawning season, say for a period of two months, all the rest of the year being open season. May and June are the usual close months, and at any other time the bass may be legally taken. But, notwithstanding the length of the open season, the character of the black bass and his habits are such that the occasions distinctly favorable for bass fishing are not numerous or of long duration. Undoubtedly the black bass is the most fished for of any American game fish, and, undoubtedly, in proportion to the number of fishermen, the annual catch is the smallest. This is because not every man who packs a fishing rod is an angler; and it is also due to the fact that the black bass is, above all, the great American "vacation" game fish, sought for very largely as a mere incident of the summer vacation, the number of men to whom the bass fishing is really a chief object being comparatively small; although, of course, among anglers, there are many who favor bass fishing above all forms of the sport.

Generally speaking, summer fishing for black bass is not overproductive. This is due to a number of causes but principally to the fact that at this time the fish are in very deep water. August, especially, is a very poor month; a succession of still, sultry days and nights is the usual thing for almost the entire month. By day the lake or river lies quiet and glassy in the blazing heat of the sun, and often the nights in the full of the moon are nearly day-light. As a consequence the bass seek the coolness to be found only in the deepest water and are distinctly off their feed. Successful bass fishing under such conditions should not be expected, and yet it is probably a fact that more bass fishing is done in August than in any other month. August is the generally accepted and duly accredited American vacation month. The summer bass angler who confines his fishing to the early morning hours, and again from sundown until dark, when the bass run into the shallows to some extent, will sometimes have fairly good sport. The bait-caster, especially, fishing early and late, may have fair success. But, however much bass fishing is done in the summer time, the angling at this time is not really satisfactory.

There are two periods in the year when bass fishing is at its best, and neither of them is of long duration. Weather being favorable, the first two or three weeks of the open season, when the bass are still generally in the rather shallow water, is a very good time to select for a bass fishing trip. Bait-casting and fly-fishing may then be depended upon for making good catches of either large- or small-mouthed bass; the bait-caster will make good scores with either surface or sinking lures, and the fly-caster, fishing in streams known to furnish good bass fly-fishing, should have no trouble in connecting with a satisfactory catch. But, as noted, this favorable time is rather short, the bass soon moving into deep water with the coming of the true summer weather. Follow then some six or seven weeks, the good old summer time, when bass angling is at its worst and the vacation fisherman at his best. And then comes the best time of all the year for bass fishing, the first few weeks in the fall, while the weather still holds comparatively warm, but the water has grown somewhat cooler.

At some time during the summer, the exact time differing with the locality, every bass lake begins to "work" or "bloom"; that is, the aquatic vegetation growing upon the lake bottom has reached maturity and begins to throw off seeds. In a short time the water takes on a milky appearance, is almost opaque, and filled with floating particles. Naturally fishing is at a standstill. Prior to this time also almost every lake becomes very weedy, the weeds eventually reaching the surface of the water along shore in the shallows and often coming within a foot or two of the surface in water from fifteen to twenty feet deep.

This makes the bass fishing rather more like raking hay than angling, and fishing at this time, especially bait- or fly-casting, is productive principally of smashed tackle and lost tempers. Later in the season, however, the lakes cease working, and the water clears; the weeds, too, die down considerably. With weather clear and just cool enough to be pleasant, the conditions generally prevailing in the early fall, with water also clear and sufficiently cool to bring the bass again into the shallows, it would appear that the first weeks of autumn, "when the bloom is off the water," are a pretty good time to go bass fishing—in fact, the very best.

To the writer it seems that, above all other methods of angling for black bass, bait-casting is to be preferred both for sport and results in fall fishing for bass. In both lakes and streams, the bass, both the large- and small-mouth, as above noted, are now in the shallower portions of lake and stream, on the bars and in the riffles, a condition decidedly favorable for bait-casting, particularly so to the bait-caster who prefers the use of the various top-water baits. With the coming of cool water the fish gain a new lease of life, an accession of activity and pugnacity, and are not at all the same fish which, in the tepid water and sultry atmosphere of July and August, required lengthy and super-skilful teasing to make them rise. The bait-caster may confidently rely for success upon any of the accepted casting baits, either surface or sinking, and the ordinary trolling spoon or single-hook fly-spoon, used in the same manner, are very successful in the fall months. The angler should look for his fish along the shelving lake shores and on the bars, and, in the streams, on point, bar, or in the riffles.

In the matter of tackle, before starting out for a bass fishing trip in the fall, the angler who has done more or less fishing during the summer should carefully test his casting line. With the best of care, it has been the writer's experience that the unwaterproofed bait-casting line of small caliber which has been in use since the opening of the bass season is not to be trusted when the season is nearing its end. It should be carefully tested and the weaker portions broken off until you have a length of good, strong line, or a visit to the tackle dealer is rendered imperative.

A weak line is not only conducive to lost fish, but is also an expensive luxury in the matter of snapping off baits. Also, the mental poise of the angler who realizes at one and the same instant that he has on the largest bass he ever saw, and that he has him on a rotten line, is not at all conducive to the calm and strategic handling of a large fish. As a general rule it is well to strengthen the tackle at all points for fall bass fishing, for at this time one is more apt to make connections with large bass than at any time during the season.

Although the preference of some anglers would certainly be for bait-casting, it is not to be understood that fly-fishing is at a discount in the autumn. The contrary is true. But the fly-caster should choose for the scene of action some well-known bass river, rather than a lake. As a general rule, with, of course, the usual exceptions necessary to prove it, fly-fishing for bass in lakes is not ordinarily a success. It is much better to select some wadable river where you can go about it in the same manner as trout fly-fishing is usually done. A canoe cruise on some good river, with bass fly-fishing as its object, in the fine weather prevailing in September and October, is a form of sport hard to equal. Since bait-casting is equally effective in either lake or river,

BAIT-CASTER AND BASSES

the canoeist may, if he chooses, depend upon his bait-casting rod for both "grub" and sport.

The fly-caster who has done most of his casting when wading would do well to practice casting from a canoe before starting out on a canoeing trip having for its object bass fly-fishing. A fact not generally recognized is that fly-casting when wading and fly-casting from a canoe are two very different propositions—you have only to try it once to admit this. It does not here seem advisable to discuss the technicalities of fly-casting from a boat or canoe; it should be noted, however, that one of the most important things is, when a cast has been made and in the retrieve, to keep a taut line from water to rod tip by stripping in the line through the guides with the left hand. It is also a good plan not to use your trout fly-rod, unless it is a very strong one, for bass fishing. The fine little trout rod, adapted to fly-casting in small streams, is ineffective and certain to be damaged if used much for bass fishing. The analogy between handling a quarter-pound brook trout and a two-pound small-mouthed bass is not at all too close for comfort.

The angler planning a trip for the fall months should remember that, while the days are sure to be comfortably warm, the nights are apt to be uncomfortably cool, and he should add to his summer camp kit, divers sweaters, blankets, etc. Also the fact that at this time it is permissible to kill waterfowl and upland game should not be overlooked, and a small-bore rifle or a shotgun, the former preferable from the canoeist's point of view, may add acceptably to the bill of fare.

The camera, too, should be taken along, for although one may not record the beautiful color schemes of an autumn day, one can still make better photographs than in mid-summer.

CHAPTER VI

THE NAMAYCUSH, THE MASCALONGE AND OTHERS

THE Great Lakes trout or namaycush trout, *Cristivomer namaycush,* and the mascalonge, *Esox masquinongy,* are the "big game" fishes of the sweet-water angler. Of the two the mascalonge is undoubtedly the better game fish but, unfortunately, far less widely distributed than the lake trout. The mascalonge also, as a surface fish, that is, for the most part inhabiting the fairly shallow water along-shore in the vicinity of the weed beds, may be fished for with more sportsmanlike tackle and methods than are practicable in the case of the namaycush, the latter being essentially a deep-water fish. Fishing for "lakers," however, when done rightly, is far from being poor sport; but the angler to get any appreciable results must know his fish and the way to fish for them. Lake trout fishing is quite unlike any other form of angling. Many lakes and ponds containing lake trout in abundance have been fished for years by anglers for bass, pike, or pickerel without so much as a strike from a laker.

Deep-trolling for the Great Lakes Trout

The angler for black bass or brook trout, or, for that matter, the canoeist or hunter—anyone who elects the early fall for his outing—would do well to include among the possibilities of his trip a try for lake trout. The necessary additions to the general outfit are not at all bulky or numerous, and where good fishing for lake trout may be had—and this is the case in numerous localities, particularly in Maine, Canada, the Adirondacks, the Berkshires, and many other regions identified with the sports of hunting and fishing—the results are such as to render the trouble of selecting and carrying the requisite tackle quite inconsiderable; moreover, while of a very special sort, the tackle for lakers is a matter of little expense.

Autumn Fishing.

The range of the Great Lakes trout, the name having reference to the Great Lakes and not, as some anglers and angling writers seem to understand it, to the size of the fish, is given by Jordan and Evermann as follows: "The namaycush trout is found in most large lakes from New Brunswick and Maine westward throughout the Great Lakes region and to Vancouver Island, thence northward to Northern Alaska, Hudson Bay, and Labrador. It is known from Henry Lake in Idaho and elsewhere in the headwaters of the Columbia. It is known also from the Fraser River basin, from Vancouver Island, and various places in Alaska."

Range.

The lake trout is so highly and justly appreciated as

a food and game fish that it is now artificially propagated by both Federal and State hatcheries and the range has accordingly increased far beyond its original limits. Stocking waters with lake trout is usually very successful and few if any failures to obtain results are reported. In every case known to the writer where the stocking was carefully and intelligently done the results have been entirely satisfactory. The lake trout is a hardy fish and its growth is fast, especially when planted in lakes not previously having these fish, since in such waters food is very abundant.

It is a noteworthy fact that many of the "big trout" stories industriously circulated every year, particularly **"Big Trout" Stories.** fish tales from Maine and Canada, are founded upon the more or less skilful and authentic capture of a good-sized lake trout on trolling tackle and not upon the taking of a brook trout, *fontinalis,* on the fly. Of course, in the waters of Maine and Canada, some very large brook trout are taken quite frequently by fly-fishermen, trout running from three to six pounds and, far less frequently, heavier than that.

Anglers who specialize on lake trout fishing consider a six-pound fish a small one. Anglers who specialize on fly-fishing for brook trout, it goes without saying, do not consider a six-pound fish a small one. Consequently, if you are a worthy and hard-working fly-caster with, as yet, a two-pound trout as your record fish, do not be unduly shocked when a friend reputedly not over-skilful in angling affairs writes you from the North Woods that he has captured an "eight-pound trout." In every case where the catch is simply hazily reported as "a trout" it is well to examine the facts before bestowing possibly unearned laurels. In some localities the lake trout is called "togue," and in others it is variously known as "lunge" (very easy to confuse with the mascalonge), "tulade," "gray trout," "Mackinaw," "laker," and "salmon trout." The lake trout should never be called a "salmon trout" for the reason stated in the following paragraph.

The lake trout is a charr, not a salmon trout, having the characteristic lack of teeth on the front of the bone in the roof of the mouth, this being the most striking difference in formation between the charr and the salmon trout.

The Namaycush a Charr.

The lake trout is a charr, a large and coarse one to be sure, when compared with the more familiar and finer-grained speckled brook trout, but, nevertheless, a charr. If your trout has teeth on both the front and rear of the roof of the mouth it is a salmon trout; if only on the rear of the mouth it is a charr.

Occasionally the lake trout attains a very large size, sometimes over one hundred pounds; but thirty pounds may be safely stated as the heaviest fish the angler may hope for. Lake trout weighing between twelve and twenty-five pounds are taken quite commonly where the fishing is ordinarily good, but the average weight of fish taken by anglers is in the vicinity of eight pounds.

Average Size.

The head and mouth of the namaycush are, proportionately, quite large, and the head is depressed, that is, rather flat. The tail is deeply forked. In colora-

NAMAYCUSH AND OTHERS

tion it is ordinarily a rather dark gray, marked profusely with spots of a lighter tinge. The head is marbled, or vermiculated, like the back of the brook trout. Occasionally the spots on the body will show a reddish shade. Generally speaking, the lake trout is a handsome and well-formed game fish, the larger specimens having length in proportion to girth. A fifteen- or sixteen-pound fish will measure about thirty-two inches.

Formation and Coloration.

It is said that the lake trout early in the spring comes into the shallows for a period of a few days when it may be taken on ordinary light tackle. However this may be—and the writer is inclined to believe that this period must be very short indeed and that in some lakes it does not occur at all—angling for lakers is done almost entirely by deep-trolling. Also it is a fact that the early season excursion of the namaycush to the surface waters is quite apt to take place before fishing for them may be done legally. In lakes where early fishing for lakers on the surface and in the shallows is an accomplished fact they may be taken on the fly as well as by trolling. Successful surface fishing is, however, a pretty rare thing, and it does not seem advisable to consider it here to any extent. For trolling heavy bass tackle will answer the purpose; and for fly-fishing a fly-rod suited to large stream and bass fly-fishing, say a ten-foot, seven-ounce rod, will be right. On this rod you should use forty yards of enameled line, size E, on a single-action reel. Flies dressed on sproat hooks numbers six and four will be sufficiently large, and

Surface Fishing.

good flies for lake trout are: royal coachman, Parmachene belle, Montreal, and silver doctor.

The lake trout is essentially a deep-water game fish, habitually seeking the very deepest portions of its habitat. It should be trolled for, therefore, in water running from fifty to one hundred feet or over in depth, preferably where the bottom is rocky, and off rocky reefs extending down into deep water. This being the case, it is not difficult to understand why anglers for bass and other fish never strike a namaycush, and also why tackle of a very specialized sort must be used in lake trout fishing. In mid-summer another good place to "work" is in the vicinity of the spring-holes. Almost every lake has its resident fisherman or fishermen—gentlemen of infinite leisure and obscure habits who "live off the lake" by fishing and guiding—who, for a suitable stipend, will reveal to you the geography of the lake bottom as regards its bars, reefs, spring-holes, etc., matters of the utmost importance to the angler for lake trout.

Where to Fish.

As for the practical side of deep-trolling, the matter of tackle, there are two methods in general use. You can use either a hand-line with a heavy sinker or you can employ a metal line, which sinks sufficiently deep by its own weight, on a fairly heavy trolling rod. The former method is distinctly the less sportsmanlike and desirable. The latter method, only recently introduced, makes a much better sport of lake trout fishing than it

Lake Trout Tackle.

NAMAYCUSH AND OTHERS

has ever been before. In detail the tackle for these two methods of fishing is as follows:

For trolling with the hand-line—in which manner it is to be regretted the greater share of lake trout fishing is still done—you will need a twisted linen line of twenty-one or twenty-four threads at least two hundred feet in length. The line, it should be stated, must be of rather large caliber in order to prevent its cutting the hands when in use. Cut off eighteen or twenty feet of the line at one end and tie in a triple action or "three-way" swivel at the point of cutting. To the third swivel tie about fifteen feet of line somewhat weaker than the main line; this is for the sinker and it must be weaker than the main line so that if the sinker is fouled the sinker line will break rather than the main line.

Use a swiveled dipsey sinker of four to eight ounces according to the depth of water. The bait and arrangement of hook or hooks will be the same as for use on a metal line and will be discussed in a later paragraph. It is a good plan to tie the sinker to the line in such a manner that when the fish has been led in close enough to the boat the sinker line may be taken into the boat and the sinker instantly and easily removed from the line by a single pull. Any simple jam-knot will make this possible.

Metal Line. The better method of deep-trolling consists in using fifty to one hundred yards of braided copper wire line on a trolling rod of suitable weight and dimensions. In this way you avoid using the heavy sinker—a thorough spoil-sport—necessary with the linen line as the weight of the metal line sinks it sufficiently deep. This line is made of a number of fine strands of copper wire braided over a silk core and should not be confused with the inferior solid copper wire lines. The braided copper line spools well on the reel, does not easily kink, and even if the latter does occur is not liable to part at the kink, no one of which things may be said for the ordinary solid copper line. Braided copper line may be had in fifty-yard spools and in two sizes, E and F, of which the smaller is the best to use in lakes of moderate depth. Size E should be used in very deep waters.

A reel is made and sold generally by the tackle dealers that is particularly adapted to deep-trolling with copper lines of the sort described above.

The Reel. This reel is single action and supplied with a strong, reliable, and easily manipulated drag; it is made of metal and is of large diameter in order that each revolution of the spindle may take up a good quantity of line. With solid copper lines—inferior, as above stated, to those of braided copper—large wooden reels, the same as used in commoner forms of saltwater fishing, are generally used. The metal reel described in this paragraph is far superior to the wooden reel and should by all means be employed for the sort of angling under discussion. Of course, any reel of large size, either double- or quadruple-multiplying, may be used. These last, however, if large enough to hold seventy-five to one hundred yards of size F braided copper line and of good quality, are rather expensive. The single-action metal reel recommended herein is quite inexpensive and also quite good enough for the purpose, it being taken for granted that deep-trolling, in all probability, will be indulged in only occasionally as a foil to your fly- or bait-casting.

In the matter of the rod any good trolling rod with a stiff backbone will answer the purpose. Its length may be from seven to eight and a quarter feet, and its material bethabara, split-bamboo, or steel. The lancewood rod is excepted because this material is apt to be too whippy. The reel-seat should be above the handgrasp. The guides of the rod should be fairly large to allow the line to run freely. German silver trumpet guides are the best for the purpose. The rod should weigh from eight to nine ounces and, as noted, should have considerable backbone in order to handle the heavy metal line, without strain. A "Henshall" casting rod in bethabara or split-bamboo and weighing eight or nine ounces will be a very good one for the purpose.

The Rod.

The leader and arrangement of hooks and bait are the same in both methods of deep-trolling with either linen or copper lines. Leaders of fine steel wire are used to some extent, but are hardly necessary. A leader of either double- or triple-twisted gut is quite strong enough for the purpose and is preferable in a good many ways to one of metal. To each end of the leader should be attached a clew-spring swivel for connection with the line and the trolling gang or artificial bait. One or two extra leaders should be carried in a soak-box.

Leaders.

For use with the natural minnow regular lake trout trolling gangs are sold by the tackle dealers consisting generally of three burrs or triple hooks and a lip-hook on gut. This number of hooks is neither imperative or sportsmanlike and, at most, it is best to use not more than the lip-hook and one treble. The gang should be tied on double gut. The natural minnow is the very best bait for lakers, and the minnows should be large, from five to seven inches in length. Brook "shiners" are the most effective. Sometimes when it is difficult to obtain minnows large enough small suckers are used, but these are not ordinarily very successful. I have even known of small brook trout being sacrificed for the purpose of trolling for lakers. It seems hardly necessary to condemn this.

Natural Baits.

In some localities it is difficult to obtain minnows in sufficient quantity or large enough for lake trout trolling and in such case resort may be had to various artificial baits. Artificial baits are not as successful with the namaycush as the natural minnow, but many good lakers are taken on them. One of the best artificials for lake trout is known as the "silver soldier." This is a minnow made of German silver, simply a flat, curved piece of metal cut in minnow-shape and fitted with a single hook. A number of trolling spoons are adapted to lake trout fishing and the best of these are the ones which do not revolve in the manner of the orthodox trolling spoon but play from side to side when drawn through the water. When deep-trolling it is often impracticable to keep the boat moving fast enough to get sufficient spin on the ordinary trolling spoon. It is also practi-

Artificial Baits.

cable to use the wooden bait-casting minnows or phantoms. Fairly large trolling spoons should be used.

A very necessary item in the kit of the angler for lake trout is a good strong gaff. The smaller trout, from four to six pounds, may be safely landed in a large landing net, if the frame and handle of the net are strong and the net itself strongly woven and firmly attached to the frame, but for the larger fish a gaff is practically imperative. On one lake where the writer trolled for lakers the local talent used frog spears in place of gaffs—four-pronged affairs something like a small pitchfork. It was somewhat amusing and rather exciting to listen to the ensuing conversation in case a poorly hooked trout was knocked off the hook when the fisherman jabbed him with the "grains" and the weapon failed to hold. On no account use one of the murderous "patent" spring gaffs. If it is desired to mount the fish as a trophy the gaff should not be used. The best alternative in case neither net or gaff is at hand and if the fish is a large one, is to shoot it through the head with a twenty-two pistol or rifle.

Gaff.

Deep-trolling requires one man at the oars and another to handle the rod. The boat should always move slowly in order that the line may run sufficiently deep and the progress of the boat should be at an even pace. When trolling with the hand-line the angler should, from time to time, "feel bottom" with the sinker to be certain that he is fishing in the proper depth of water. As above noted the trolling should be done along the deep chan-

Practical Hints.

nels, over spring-holes, and where the bottom is rocky.

When a fish is struck it should not be hurried into the boat but played in gradually. As a usual thing, particularly when a hand-line is used, the lake trout will do most of his fighting after being brought within sight of the boat. It will then make swift rushes from side to side or again bore steadily down into deep water. At such times line should be freely given the trout, not reeling in again until the fish stops running or sounding. The fish should never be landed until it is thoroughly played to a finish—a namaycush of good size if prematurely taken into the boat while it is still full of fight will make things exceedingly interesting for the occupants of the craft.

The method of deep-trolling with metal lines, with certain variations of tackle to suit the occasion, may be used for other game fishes than the namaycush in the summer months when the hot weather has driven most of them to the deep water—and used with success.

The Mascalonge, Pike, and Pickerel

Of the pike family (*Esocidae*) three members claim the attention of anglers, namely, the mascalonge, *Esox masquinongy,* the pike, *Esox lucius,* and the Eastern pickerel, *Esox reticulatus.* In England, pike fishing is far more popular than in America. Of the three fishes mentioned the mascalonge is the only one which receives the serious attention of the American angler, and even this fine game fish, owing to its somewhat restricted range, is well-known and regularly fished for by comparatively few anglers. Probably the most accessible place for the Eastern angler who wishes to have a try at the mascalonge is Chautauqua Lake in New York where the unspotted mascalonge, *Esox ohiensis,* is somewhat abundant.

Undoubtedly were it not for the black bass, a game fish unknown to the English angler, fishing for the various members of the pike family, particularly the mascalonge and Great Lakes pike, would be far more popular in this country and more seriously undertaken, quite as much so as in England. As a matter of fact, the mascalonge, of course, the pike, and even the pickerel are worthy of any angler's steel. But the extensive range of the large- and small-mouthed black bass, and their undoubted game qualities, to say nothing of the various species of brook trout, serve to relegate the pike and pickerel to the class of less-desirables, while the comparative scarcity and inaccessibility of good mascalonge waters tend to keep this fish—by many considered the gamest and the finest fish of American fresh-waters—in the background.

Although individually the most important members of the pike family differ greatly, treated collectively, their habits are much the same. All are shoal-water fishes, "using" principally in the weed beds along-shore and on the bars of lake or river; all are habitually and most destructively piscivorous, always seeking whom they may devour. Owing to the similarity of habits angling for mascalonge, pike, or pickerel differs intrinsically more in means than in ways—the methods employed are quite similar, the tackle varying to suit the occasion and the quarry.

Scientific details concerning the range, formation, coloration, and other matters dealing with the natural history of the pike family, have been very fully given in almost every angling book, while the more practical phase of the subject, the question of methods and tackle, has not been so completely treated. For this reason it would seem well to confine the present discussion principally to the ways and means of fishing for the mascalonge and its lesser relatives in preference to rehearsing again the already thoroughly detailed nature and life histories of the game fishes mentioned.

For either mascalonge, pike, or pickerel—it seems a little improper to thus class the pickerel, or, for that matter, the pike, with the mascalonge, but the fact remains that they are "birds" of the same feather—still-fishing is little done by those who understand the game. It is far better to fish exclusively by casting or trolling. The boat, when trolling, should be worked so that the bait, either artificial or natural, plays along from three to six or eight feet outside the line of weeds or rushes, and it is not necessary that the spoon or minnow be fished at any considerable depth; surface or near-surface fishing is the rule with any of these fish as they will all rise freely on seeing the bait.

When casting, the boat should travel parallel with the margin of the weed beds, from forty to eighty feet away—it depends somewhat upon the skill of the caster and the method of casting—and the bait should be cast in so as to fall at the proper distance from the weeds, taking pains not to cast so far in as to become fouled in the weeds or so far away from them as to render it problematical whether the fish will see the bait. In either case as soon as a fish is hooked the boatman should make it a point to keep the boat in deep water; the fish should always be played away from the weeds.

Mascalonge weighing over twenty pounds have been taken on five-ounce split-cane bass-casting rods, using a small caliber bait-casting line and a light quadruple multiplying reel with a small sized single-hook casting spoon for the lure. On the other hand mascalonge anglers, as a rule, do not belong to the light-tackle brigade; hand-lines or heavy steel rods equipped with line, reel, and spoon correspondingly large and weighty seem to be the rule. The average angler, possessing average skill in tackle-handling and an average sense of the due proportions of things, together with a modicum of insight as to the difference between angling and pot-fishing, will do well to strike a happy medium.

For either casting or trolling for mascalonge a good grade split-bamboo rod, from seven to eight feet three inches in length, weighing from eight to nine ounces, will answer the purpose, always provided it is handled with the necessary dexterity. The rod should be equipped with trumpet guides of German silver, or steel wire guides, using preferably agates for the hand- and tip-guides; the reel-seat, having one of the numerous forms of locking attachments, must be above the hand-grasp.

For trolling, a double-multiplying reel should be used as it has more winding-in power than a quadruple multiplier, but for casting a four-multiplier is, of course, imperative. The trolling line may well be waterproofed, but for casting an undressed line must be used, size E or F for mascalonge and large pike, size G for pickerel. For pickerel the rods, reels, and lines used for bass bait-casting and trolling are right.

Baits of exceedingly various sorts are used for mascalonge and pike, minnows natural and artificial, frogs, spoons, and spinners, and some of the floating baits for bass, the last made larger and stronger for mascalonge fishing, but the most effective are a large natural minnow or a common trolling spoon size four or five. A steel wire leader should always be used. Gimp leaders rot inside and will smash without warning visible to the angler. In case a spinning bait is used, such as the Archer spinner with minnow, frog, or pork-rind, use a swivel gang composed of six or eight medium sized bronze barrel swivels, or a trolling "keel" or "coin" sinker, the last being a round, flat sinker the size and shape of a five-cent piece which, when bent on the line, forms a keel that effectually prevents the line from twisting and kinking. Another device to prevent line-kinking is known as the "Pilot"; this may be used also to cause the bait to run at will on the surface or considerably submerged.

As both mascalonge and pike are very large fish it is necessary to use a gaff in landing them. If the writer is not greatly mistaken he has more than once seen the common pickerel, fairly large as these fish run on the average, leap on a practically slack line, although tactics of this sort are not ordinarily ascribed to this fish. It is fairly well known that the mascalonge is a "jumper from Jumperville." Sportsmen are apt to disagree as to the proper rod move to make when a game fish takes the air. The preponderance of experience and advice suggests the advisability of slightly lowering the rod tip. Usually, unless the angler is very cool and also a rapid thinker with a very swift reaction from brain to hand, the fish, salmon, black bass, or musky as the case may be, is back in the water before the angler makes any counter play at all. However, it is always best to ease a leaping fish back into the water by slightly lowering the tip. When a fish leaps far away from the boat, lowering the tip is perfectly useless as there is always a long belly in the line and the movement of the rod does not carry through.

Anglers often find it difficult correctly to differentiate a large pike from a mascalonge (in some cases, possibly, because the wish is father to the thought), or, say, an unusually large pickerel from a pike. The following key, quoted from Dr. James A. Henshall, will afford the means of rightly identifying and distinguishing the most fished-for members of the pike family.

"The mascalonge has the upper part of both the cheeks and gill-covers scaly, while the lower half of both cheeks and gill-covers is naked; it has from seventeen to nineteen branchiostegal rays (the branchiostegals are the rays on the under side of the gill-cover, that, like the ribs of an umbrella, assist in opening and closing it during breathing). Its coloration is of a uniform grayish hue, or when marked with spots or bars they are always of a much darker color or shade than the ground color.

"The pike has the cheeks entirely scaly, but only the upper part of the gill-cover, the lower half being naked; it has from fourteen to sixteen branchiostegal rays; its coloration is a bluish or greenish gray, with elongated or bean-shaped spots covering the sides, which are always of a lighter hue than the ground color.

"The Eastern or reticulated pickerel has both the cheeks and gill-covers entirely covered with scales; it has from fourteen to sixteen branchiostegal rays; its coloration is shades of green, with sides of golden luster, and marked with dark reticulations, mostly horizontal. It is rarely or never found west of the Alleghanies."

The Ouananiche and Land-locked Salmon

The Atlantic salmon, *Salmo salar,* has two land-locked relatives, the "land-locked salmon" proper, *Salmo sebago,* and the ouananiche, *Salmo ouananiche.* Many experienced anglers believe that there is no essential difference between the Sebago salmon and the ouananiche, or between these two and the sea salmon. However this may be—and the authorities, Jordan and Evermann, who some years ago thus classified them ("for the present") have not as yet published a contrary opinion—it is not of extreme importance to the angler; the fact remains that both the land-locked salmon and the ouananiche are, as game fishes, in the very first flight.

The land-locked salmon is found in many of the lakes of Maine and by fish cultural operations its range is constantly increasing. It was originally described from Sebago Lake. Fly-fishing for land-locked salmon may be had at Grand Lake Stream in Maine, and, for the ouananiche, at the Grand Decharge of the Saguenay River which flows from Lake St. John, Province of Quebec, Canada. In Grand Lake, other Maine lakes, and in Lake St. John the fishing is chiefly done by trolling.

For either fly-casting or trolling for land-locks and ouananiche heavy trout tackle is suitable, although where the fish run large a grilse rod may be used. Land-locked salmon taken by trolling in lakes weigh from eight to twenty pounds. Those taken by fly-fishing in streams, as in Grand Lake Stream and at the Grand Decharge, average two pounds and seldom range over five. Small sized salmon flies are generally used. Latterly, at Grand Lake Stream, dry-fly fishing for land-locks has been tried successfully when the wet-fly fishing with the larger flies has been below par.

The following narrative of the capture of a land-locked salmon on fly-tackle at Grand Lake (by the present writer considered the very best "fish story" he has ever had the pleasure of reading—for which reason the somewhat lengthy quotation is, perhaps, pardonable), written by Mr. Henry Wysham Lanier and published in *The Outing Magazine,* July, 1903, under the title of "The Gamest Fish That Swims," will afford the best possible idea of the character of the land-locked salmon, when taken in running water, or of the ouananiche, and of the tackle and methods employed. The reader particularly interested in the land-locked salmon and the ouananiche, should not fail to read the entire article of which only a small part is here quoted.

" 'Now, den, just give two, tree cast in de cunal first,' said Peter the Dane.

"It was half-past five of a June morning—June by the calendar, early April by the cold blast that swept down out of the north across the lake. Peter had put together the stiff five-and-a-half ounce bamboo, carefully soaked out a six-foot single leader, and rigged up a cast of a Jock Scott and a professor on number five Sproat hooks. On the reel were seventy-five yards of waterproof silk line, size E, as the rod had plenty of backbone and casting in such a wind needed all the helps possible.

"I stepped up to the canal, a thirty-foot runway from the lake which once fed the abandoned saw-mill, and cast down the gently eddying stream. When I had gotten out thirty or forty feet of line, working the flies lightly across the surface as they swung with the current, Peter grunted approval.

" 'I gass you do ahl right. We go out in de cunoe.'

"I may not have mentioned the fact that Peter is a guide of unusual intelligence; his knowledge of lures and of the baffling habits of the *Salmonidae* is unexcelled; nor is his horizon, by any means, bounded by fish. We stepped simultaneously into the canoe and into an atmosphere of good fellowship.

"A few strokes of the paddle sent us out to the line of triangular log cribs marking the hundred-yard limit above the dam, within which only fly-fishing is permitted; and, tying up to a buoy in eight or ten feet of water, we swung around with the wind to a north and south position not more than fifty yards from the tumbledown dock that lined the shore along the head of the canal.

"The lately risen sun shone brightly, except when a mass of gray-white clouds drove across it; the waves tossed the little cedar canoe airily up and down; on the rising shore the fresh green of the white-stemmed birches stood out sharply against the dark spruce trees, the feathery blue-green of the pines, and the rusty yellow-green of the young cedars and alders. A wild duck and her fluffy brood paddled about furtively beneath the bushes fringing the shore two hundred yards away; in the cleared spaces on the bank sleek robins, with aldermanic vests of red and inquisitive yellow beaks, hopped about among the buttercups and daisies and wild roses; while a song-sparrow poured out a full-throated trill from a neighboring fence-post.

"It must be confessed, however, that these beauties of nature, the Indian's shack cresting the bare hill, the group of little, unpainted dwelling houses, and the dozen forlorn, uniform, empty gray cabins where once lived the workers in the deserted tannery—even the sky-piercing brick chimney itself, such a strange sight in the deep woods—made but a vague impression upon my senses. For when Piscator has been casting flies in imagination only, for eleven months from a revolving office chair, he is not to be diverted by such trifles from his first lust of fish.

"I began to cast out toward the shore, tip well down to the water each time on account of the wind. After covering the leeward semi-circle fifteen or twenty times, my inexperience fancied that region tested of salmon; no trout or bass fisherman would have bothered with it longer; but since Peter made no sign I kept on casting. When the inevitable slackness of interest had drawn my eyes to the two canoes by the outlet, the occupants of which were switching away as industriously as myself, something happened—and heart came into mouth with a leap; for as the flies jiggled in over the tossing water there was a boil and swirl by the dropper, not twenty-five feet away, and a simultaneous exclamation from behind: 'Don't leave it; cast again. Dat excite him when de fly come again.'

"Shortening the cast, I sent the flies hastily and awkwardly ten feet beyond the danger signal. Hardly had they begun to come in when there was a sudden commotion; an instinctive 'strike' met a line taut and suddenly endowed with life; and the little rod bowed its acknowledgments at the meeting.

"First came a mad rush to one side, and after giving the mysterious visitor all the line that had been stripped with the left hand, I snubbed him, in order to have a feel of him. The result was immediate and surprising. Three feet into the air came a twenty-inch bow of silver, flashing in the morning sun as the salmon tried to shake himself free. Down went the tip, but, with the training of the black bass fisherman, I tried to cant him to one side and upset him before he could shake himself.

"'Don't do dat!' called watchful Peter. 'De salmon mout' is tender. You can't treat him lak black bass. Drop de tip straight toward him and den tighten up de instant he touch de water.'

"As he spoke, out came his royal highness again, and the rod dropped to greet him, for that spring and lashing out against a taut line must mean either a lost fish or a broken tip.

"'A good fish,' said Peter the Dane. 'T'ree pound strong.'

"And indeed it was the strongest three pounds the little rod had ever tried conclusions with. Hardly had he touched the water and the pressure been resumed when he was into the air once more, so far away that the eye almost refused to believe it the same fish. When he reached the surface this time he danced ten feet away on his tail, disappeared with a swoop that set the reel to singing a valkyr's shriek, and was out twice more in rapid succession, somersaulting till the air seemed full of salmon.

"These acrobatic displays and the continued strain of the sturdy bamboo were taking the edge off his fierceness. A dozen feet of the line came onto the reel before he fairly realized any compulsion. 'What, done already?' But at that instant the reel handle began to revolve the other way and no other answer was needed. Around the canoe he dashed, the line cutting through the water with that swish so dear to the heart of the angler. A little snubbing brought him up for the fifth leap, and then followed darts and rushes in every direction, and savage tugs and shakes and borings downward, and circus-like gallops round and round, while his burnished sides sent up old gold flashes through the clear but dark-colored water.

"'Keep de butt down,' cautioned my mentor. 'Don't never give him straight rod excep' when he jump, and den put strain on him again right off,' and Peter leaned toward me, almost whispering in his anxiety.

"There had been considerable strain on him already, judging from the feel of my wrist, but I let him have the full curve, and in a few minutes more this began to take effect. Slowly reeling in and fighting for every yard, the fish was brought within ten feet of the canoe; then the sight of us and the net started him off again, and it was all to do over. Gradually he was forced toward us, swinging in and out time after time, till at last he lay for a breathless instant within three feet of the gunwale, getting up courage for another spurt. With a dexterous sweep, Peter brought the landing net up behind—and his salmonship's next wild struggles were against its meshes in the bottom of the canoe.

"It was a beautiful creature that threw itself frantically about, flopping from side to side, bending double and lashing out with surprising strength, and springing violently into the air, net and all. About twenty inches long, stocky and well-rounded, but perfectly proportioned, with savage head and jaws, he seemed built for doughty deeds and the strenuous life. His back was a rich velvety green, lustrous from the glistening water and covered with half-concealed black spots. This color gradually shaded into a lighter tint, merging at the median line into a silvery coat that gleamed roseate and iridescent in the sunlight."

CHAPTER VII

FINE AND FAR-OFF FISHING AND OTHER MATTERS

FISHING "fine and far-off" is a phrase rather over-worked in the literature of fly-casting and, moreover, one which we somewhat rarely see put into actual practice on stream or lake. The rarity of really fine and far-off fishing—the words being applicable only to fly-fishing, and more especially to the act of casting the fly—is easily explained. Far casting demands the best of skill and tackle, and fine fishing, in addition to the requirements of light leaders and small flies, calls for extreme accuracy and delicacy in laying down leader and flies far-off on the water. To attain to fine and far casting and fly-fishing the angler must have the best of rods, a line entirely suited to being cast by that rod, leader and fly-snells working well together and both in keeping with the line in use; also there is requisite the skill in casting resulting from long practice and, it must be admitted, natural ability in that direction. Expert fly-casting is natural to some men just as skilful wing-shooting is to others. So we do not see very much fishing fine and far-off.

The everyday fly-fisherman contents himself with short-distance casting and does not sufficiently refine his tackle to make far-casting possible, even if his wrist were equal to the occasion. And quite often the man who owns the finest and most expensive rods, rods made with the utmost manual skill for the express purpose of better-than-average fly-casting, fishes with bait. It is not often that we find an angler whose tackle, skill, stream knowledge, and experience are adequate to the sort of casting and fishing under discussion. And yet at some time on every trout stream, and on some streams at all times, fine and far-casting are imperative for success; and it would seem that no enthusiastic fly-caster should rest satisfied with his tackle and methods until both have been brought to the point where long and delicate casting is within his power. With a view to italicizing the fact that skilled rod handling and discriminating tackle selection have their sure reward, certain times and places are noted in the following paragraphs where and when casting fine and far-off is either advantageous or imperative.

Generally speaking, the time when a long line and delicate leader and flies are most in demand is in the late spring and summer; not always, of course, even at this time, because the stream is frequently replenished by rains. But when very low and crystal clear water prevails, when a gut leader of average caliber looks on the surface of the water or beneath it like the Atlantic cable, and when the brook trout, poised in the shallow riffles, seem to see the angler for half a mile, then the man who can compass reasonable, not tournament, long-distance casts, and who understands and appreciates the killing qualities of the ephemeral leader and the almost infinitesimal fly is in his element. And who would deny that one trout taken under such conditions, by virtue of skilled casting and fine tackle, is worth vastly more than a dozen taken by chuck-and-chance-it short-line casting under easier circumstances?

It should, however, be said that the long cast, under dry weather conditions, if the angler will keep himself out of sight, is not so important as the use of small flies and fine leaders. A friend of the writer's is a very successful low-water fisherman, and yet I do not think that he ever put out over forty feet of line in his life; but when the stage of the water and the shyness of the trout require it he invariably uses midge flies and the finest of fine leaders, in the employment of which he is passing skilful—and keeps out of sight. I have seen this angler fish through a meadow where no brush screened the brook, behind two other fly-casters, and come out with several good fish when the two men who preceded him took nothing. Progress for the most part on "hands and knees," a fine and long leader, and midge flies did the trick; and, by the way, something besides pile-driver methods are necessary if you would rise, strike, and land a good trout on a midge. Frequently, however, keeping out of sight is impossible, or a matter of too much difficulty, and then long casting is the only thing.

In summer, during the day, pool fishing is very apt to be productive. Then the trout haunt the deep, dark pools, well shaded, or the reaches of equally peaceful and shady still-waters. To fish such a place with success demands every bit of skill even the veteran fly-caster can command; to the beginner such places are sloughs of despond rather than likely trout pools. On still days the surface of the pool, unruffled by any breeze, is so smooth and quiet that the disturbance of a natural insect falling upon it is very appreciable; when the ambitious but unskilled fly-caster drops his cast of flies thereon the result is simply a tidal wave.

Summer Pool Fishing.

It is small wonder that the average angler passes up the quiet pools and still-waters as unproductive—they are so except to the man who through years of stream experience and by virtue of superior casting and tackle can really fish fine and far-off. For such a man the pools and still-waters hold prizes well worth the utmost exercise of his skill, for of all stream localities it is well known that the deep pool and the dark still-water are most apt to shelter Leviathan. Small flies, light leaders, and long, light casting are the requisites for summer pool fishing. There is one thing more: Keep out of sight. Pool fishing in general and the use of dry-flies in connection therewith have been discussed elsewhere.

Apart from summer fly-fishing, under dry weather conditions, several other situations will occur to the experienced angler as calling for a long line and accurate and delicate handling. To revert for a moment to pool fishing, it may be said that a large pool, in the average rocky and forest-margined trout stream, at all times requires far-casting if you would get the most out of it—mean-

Fishing the Swift Pool.

FINE AND FAR-OFF FISHING

ing possibly a three-pounder. Starting to cast with two things in mind, that many times the pool is best fished up-stream and that, other things being equal, a short line is always safest, the angler will cover all available water with a moderate length of line, and then, picking out some vantage-point where the back cast may be made with the greatest assurance that it will not hang-up, he will whip the far-off places where his stream experience hints that a trout may be lying.

The angler of limited casting ability is distinctly handicapped when it comes to fishing a large pool. Furthermore it is a fact that the ability to get out a long line, although with entire lack of delicacy, and though the flies hit the water as if shot from a rifle, is far better than not to be able to handle anything but a short line; for, many times, the character of the pool will be such that distance and fair accuracy are the only requisites. In a pool of broken, swirling water, foam-covered and swift, it makes little difference whether the flies come down lightly or not. When fishing this sort of water the submerged fly is the proper thing, and the situation demands only the ability, by strong-arm methods or in any other way, to get out the line far enough.

Fly-fishing for trout is usually and properly associated with swift and rocky streams. We are told by the scientists that the nature of the brook trout requires highly aerated water such as the typical trout stream with its alternating riffles, rapids, and falls affords. But the experienced fly-caster can doubtless remember

Fishing Sluggish Streams.

the time when his flies were cast over the waters of some sluggish, dark-bottomed stream, almost currentless, and cast, possibly, with success. It is a fact that trout streams of this sort are quite common, and usually the trout therein are uncommonly large, although they may not be very numerous. Such streams are many times found in swamps or running through cleared fields adjacent to swampy lowlands. Here again fine and far casting is at a premium.

Usually such streams are suited to fly-casting only where they run through clearings and meadow lands, where the banks afford no ambush and the surface of the water is smooth and quiet. It is necessary to stand well away from the bank and swing a long line to reach the best of the water without alarming the fish, and the flies and leader must fall "straight" and without the suspicion of a splash. Over water of this sort the retrieve should be made slowly, even, at times, allowing the flies to become wholly submerged; otherwise there is too much fuss made on the water in bringing in the fly.

Casting from a canoe or boat over the quiet waters of a lake is another situation calling for expert handling of rod and line. Except on extraordinary occasions the angler who, within reason and without neglecting good water more easily fished, can cast farthest from the boat will be most successful. Here, as in all long-distance casting, the thing to remember is not to carry the rod too far backward on the back cast. The rod, as before noted, should not go back much beyond the

Casting from a Canoe.

perpendicular; the thing to aim for is a high back cast.

Successful fly-casting fine and far-off requires, however, something more than the ability to get out a long line and lay it down straight and softly.

Striking with a Long Line. The angler must be able to strike his trout without over-many misses and also to play him, both at the end of a long line. Consistently successful striking at long distances is, in addition to the usual requirements of quick eye and snappy wrist, purely dependent upon a taut line. An actually taut line, however, is not possible when distance casting; more or less sag is bound to occur in proportion to the rate at which the line is stripped in and the backward motion of the rod. Striking, when a long line is out, should therefore be done with more force, quicker than when using a short line. The backward motion of the rod must first take up the slack line before sufficient draw is imparted to the hook to set it firmly.

Fly-fishing fine and far-off is a pretty difficult game to play successfully—a game of skill purely and one, moreover, at which every fly-fisherman should strive to become expert—in spite of the fact that in this respect the expression "many are called but few are chosen" holds true as well as in any other branch of sport in which the highest form of skill and greatest amount of experience are required.

Fly- and Bait-casting for Accuracy, Delicacy, and Distance

These are terms which, while very familiar to tournament fly- and bait-casters, are seldom heard among anglers in general. However this may be, with the possible exception of distance—and that this at times is also very necessary has been pointed out—the success of the bait- or fly-caster in actual fishing is greatly dependent upon the degree of skill to which he has attained in regard to these three casting requisites.

The fisherman who can only approximately reach the spot where he desires to place a bait, or who so **Accuracy.** handles a cast of flies that they drop two or three feet away from the point aimed for is distinctly handicapped. In both black bass and trout fishing absolute accuracy, that is, accuracy as far as it may reasonably be attained, is a necessity for the very simple reason that both bass and trout are so constituted that very frequently they will only strike a fly or bait when it is presented to them in a certain way and in a certain spot. The angler for large-mouthed bass, when fishing along a patch of water weeds or rushes, has ample opportunity to verify this statement. He finds that if the bait drops too far away from the rushes or too close to them the bass will not rise. For success the bait must be cast so as to strike the water at a certain distance from the weeds, and the allowance for deviation is very slight.

Frequently when bass fishing you will see a bass jump within casting distance from the canoe. Then, if you can immediately drop your bait plump in the middle of the widening circle of ripples, the bass is generally yours. But if your bait strikes only somewhere near the place the chances are that the fish will stay in the water. Also it is often necessary when the bass are lying in the weeds to cast the bait into the small openings of clear water that are found here and there. This, of course, is when the weeds have grown so as to reach the surface of the water, a condition which prevails very generally during the summer. However, since under these conditions it is most often necessary for safety in landing the fish to use a rather short line, accuracy in this particular instance is not difficult.

In fly-fishing for trout accuracy is even more imperative than in bait-casting. Time and time again the writer has experimented in regard to this. It is an absolute fact that at times a trout will not rise if the fly varies only a matter of a very few inches from where he wants it. The fish will rise when the fly reaches a certain spot; if it varies almost infinitesimally—say three inches—the fish will stay down. But it is not only in this regard that accuracy in casting is desirable. The banks of most of our best trout streams are more or less, generally more, wooded and brush-grown and overhanging branches must continually be taken into consideration. The man who lacks accurate control over his line both in the forward and back casts is always in hot water, although he may be fishing "the icy waters of a mountain trout brook."

Delicacy in bait-casting is a thing attained only with much practice. An artificial minnow or spoon, with from seventy-five to a hundred feet of line out, is bound to hit the water with considerable force. Strange as it may seem, this as a rule does not alarm the fish. But in fishing very shallow water along-shore, or in reedy river coves where the water is not deep, care must be taken in this particular. If you succeed in starting the minnow toward the rod just before or at the instant it strikes the water, reasonable delicacy results. A great many bait-casters are careless in this regard with the natural consequence that their success is not phenomenal. If, at the end of the cast, the bait lies for an instant motionless and dead on the water, a bass whose interest has been aroused to the point of striking will usually change his mind. I have, however, several times seen bass strike a bait floating "dead" on the surface while the angler was arguing with his reel the question whether a backlash is merely a misfortune or an actual calamity. This, of course, is very exceptional; the motion of the lure is the factor that brings the strikes.

Delicacy.

In fly-casting, delicacy to a certain degree is not difficult of attainment. Beyond that certain degree, with which no fly-caster should be satisfied, it is a matter of no little difficulty and requires years of stream experience and practice. When fishing the clear, shallow riffles of small streams the flies must drop on the water with the lightness of the proverbial thistle-down. If you fail in this you will see the trout in that vicinity disappear with uniform celerity. It is when casting a long line that the veteran fly-caster, by the ease with which he causes the flies to alight straight, delicately, and far-off, shows his title to the degree of Master of Angling. An equal degree of skill should be the goal of every fly-caster.

A rising motion of the rod just before the flies are about to alight will cause them to land quietly. This motion of the rod, however, must not be sudden or jerky, but must be graduated with nicety; otherwise the process simply results in "snapping the whip" and the flies will strike the water with even more than ordinary force. Another factor in casting for delicacy is to aim not at the exact spot on the water where the flies should alight but at a point in the air four or five feet above the spot. This will cause leader and flies to straighten out in the air, lose in a measure the propulsive force of the cast, and fall with all necessary delicacy.

Distance. Distance in both fly- and bait-casting, although at times very necessary, is generally of less importance than accuracy and delicacy. It is an angling axiom that the more line you have out the better are your chances for failing to hook a rising fish, or, if the fish is struck, of eventually losing him. It is always advisable to use the shortest line permissible under the circumstances. By so doing accuracy and delicacy are more easily and surely attained, you have more control over the strike, and instant control over a fish when struck.

The chief advantage of distance comes when, owing to the natural conformation of the pond or stream, or to the extreme shyness of the fish, lengthening out is rendered imperative. The practice of distance casting is, however, of distinct advantage, for the reason that the man who can skilfully handle a long line can still more skilfully handle a short one. The angler should, nevertheless, never allow the obsession of distance to get the better of him. Unless you have a very natural aptitude, gaining distance is rather a slow process. It is much better to confine yourself to the correct handling of moderate casts and let distance take care of itself. In due time a fairly long line comes automatically.

How to Improve the Fly-rod

Satisfactory fly-casting under any conditions exacts the finest possible adjustment of tackle in every way; but, chiefly, the rod must be a good one and its furniture capable of giving the results which the caster desires. If your casting to-date is not as good as it should be it is quite possible that the rod is at fault. It might be suggested that before you make up your mind that you are a born duffer at the game you first make sure that the tools you have been using are suited to it. A good fly-rod need not be expensive, while, at the same time, it cannot be cheap. Granted that the material is of fairly good quality, it may be said that effective casting depends greatly upon the style of guides, the balance, the method of winding, etc., things which to a certain extent may be regulated at will without going to the expense of a new rod. Buying a fly-rod is always a pleasure but sometimes, unfortunately, the state of the money market is prohibitive.

If originally the rod was a good one as regards material, of carefully selected and assembled cane if the rod is a split-bamboo, or of well-seasoned bethabara, lancewood, or greenheart if a solid-wood, almost any old rod may be made pretty nearly as good as new—in many cases much better than new—by its owner, who, moreover, need not be a mechanical genius or the proprietor of a machine shop. Ingenuity, elbow-grease, a few simple tools, and chiefly a knowledge of what constitutes a good fly-rod are practically the only essentials. Furthermore, if you have not the time or do not care to do these things yourself it will be of advantage to you to be able to tell the professional rod maker exactly the things you wish done.

Often a rod will show a quality of whippiness which was not suspected when the rod was purchased. Provided you are not an advocate of the **The Whippy Rod.** whippy rod—there are such and they are more to be pitied than censured—with the knowledge that you have on your hands an unsatisfactory tool comes the realization of the necessity of a new rod or a radical improvement in the present one. The extent of the change necessary is dependent upon the degree of softness with which the rod is afflicted. The rod repairer in this particular instance, if the rod is only slightly whippy, will remove all the windings and replace them at closer intervals; or, possibly, the addition of new windings between those already on the rod will do just as well. The average fly-rod is wound at intervals of slightly over an inch. Windings at only one-half inch will stiffen the rod appreciably. If, however, in the opinion of the repairer, the extreme softness of the rod demands more radical treatment resort may be had to amputation. In the case of the average fly-rod, consisting of three joints and from nine to ten feet long, at least one inch should be removed from each joint; to further insure successful results it might be well to put on additional windings. The resulting difference in the action of the rod is very great, while the loss of weight is so slight as to be negligible.

In this connection it should be added that winding the rod entirely from end to end, called solid winding, should not be done. At first glance, considering the fact that additional windings stiffen the rod, one would naturally conclude that the solid wound rod is a very stiff one. This is not the case, however. Solid wound rods tend to be soft rather than otherwise and the method is not approved or followed by the best rod makers.

The angler whose ambition lies along the line of distance casting will find that he can easily lengthen out his average casting by replacing the ring-and-keeper guides with which his rod is fitted with the now more popular and far more efficient English snake guides. The old-fashioned ring-and-keeper guides are not very well adapted to shooting the line, the loosely working ring and its generally small aperture causing too much friction. The snake guide, as in the case of much fly-tackle, is an English idea. Their stability and line shooting adaptability are far in advance of the ring guides, and, moreover, the snake guides measurably facilitate stringing-up the rod and are less liable to become bent out of shape. Of the snake guides those of steel are best.

German silver is also a good material but inferior to steel for the reason that it is softer and the line soon wears grooves in the guides. If you wish to go a bit farther, with the idea of having the rod thoroughly modern and efficient in the matter of guides, fit it with offset agate tip guide and raised agate hand guide. Then if you do not do good casting, you certainly cannot, provided the rod itself is fairly good, "blame the gun."

If the rod is heavy in hand, it may be made a sweeter rod to handle by removing the solid metal reel-seat in favor of plain reel-bands; if the handgrasp is of wood or celluloid a further reduction in weight may be effected by fitting a solid cork grasp. On general principles any rod which has a handgrasp of cork sheathing over a shaped core of wood may be made a much better rod by the substitution of a solid cork grasp in place of the cheaper and far less durable and desirable grasp of thin cork over wood. The solid cork grasp is made of a number of disks of solid cork fitted over a core.

Butt and Top Heavy Rods.

On the other hand, the top-heavy rod may be made to balance much better by simply using on it a heavier reel. The slightly top-heavy rod is not objectionable to a good many anglers, and often a rod of this sort is a very strong caster. The famous Castle Connell salmon rods are made on this principle. Such a rod is, however, apt to be tiring in long continued casting, and the average angler prefers a well balanced rod just as a rifleman desires this quality in his weapon.

If the rod is too stiff there is only one thing to do unless you are an expert rod maker, and barring a trip to the professional rod repairer, and that is: Use a heavy line. The chances are that if the rod does not weigh over five ounces a level line, size E, will bring out all the action desirable, while a line of size F or G may fail entirely to do so. The suitability of the line to the rod upon which it is used is a matter which many anglers do not sufficiently consider. To state the extreme, the fly-caster who uses on a three-and-a-half-ounce fly-rod a line of size E and the caster who uses on a ten-foot seven-ounce rod a line of size G will find that good casting with such ill-assorted tackle is impossible.

The Stiff Rod.

A heavy line is too burdensome for the featherweight fly-rod; in fact, if the angler is inclined to be heavy-handed, it is quite possible for him to smash the rod by attempting to use a too heavy line upon it. Similarly, a fairly long cast, using a very light line on a comparatively heavy rod, is not possible; the line must have sufficient weight to carry it through the air in response to force of the cast. But in the case of a very stiff rod, the weight of a heavy line will produce much more snap and bend in the rod, and although the combination makes the work rather strenuous, still it is very efficient. It is hardly necessary to state that such an outfit would, however, be very poorly adapted to small stream work.

The repair of smashed rods does not properly come under the subject we are discussing—it is fairly obvious that any smashed rod, when repaired, is considerably improved—but the best way to cure a rod that has acquired a more or less decided "set" may properly be noted. The set may be the result of strain or warp, the first due to overburdening the rod in some way and the last to poor material—in which case a permanent cure can hardly be effected—or to negligence. This is a case where an ounce of prevention is sometimes worth six ounces of good fly-rod, and before noting the method of correction it might be well to set down a few golden rules about the way not to use a fly-rod.

The Way Not to Use a Fly-rod.

In the first place since the fly-rod forms our subject—although most of these suggestions are equally applicable to fishing rods in general—it should be said that the split-cane rod is peculiarly, often fatally, susceptible to dampness, and that consequently every precaution should be taken in this regard. In camp it should be taken down and put in the case over-night and certainly should never be left lying on the ground for any length of time. It is quite possible to put a fine split-bamboo fly-rod temporarily or even permanently out of commission by allowing it to lie out over-night on the ground. Again, to avoid warp, the rod when assembled should never be leaned against a support in such a manner as to bend it. If left for a sufficient length of time, not necessarily a very long time, leaning in this way the bend will become permanent. Similarly, when the rod is unjointed, the individual joints should not be leaned against a support in the manner noted, for the same reason.

The remedy and the method of prevention for warp

or set are quite similar. The rod which has acquired a set should be hung up by the tip with a weight attached to the butt, provided the set runs through the entire rod; if only one joint is affected this should be treated in the same manner. By way of prevention when the rod is to be unused for a long time, as during the winter months, suspending each joint separately, or at least the tip and middle joints, is by far the best way of storing it. If you have a rod and gun cabinet it is exactly suited to the purpose. When the rod is suspended merely as a matter of precaution it is unnecessary to use a weight.

The Remedy for "Set."

The man who makes his own rods certainly derives more pleasure from their use than does the angler who uses a ready-made rod—this in spite of the fact that the professionally made rod will always be the better one unless the amateur maker is very expert indeed. In due proportion, there is more sport in handling a rod the efficiency of which is partly due to your own tinkering than in using one upon which you have no claim for improvements.

Strip-casting for Black Bass

If you have never learned bait-casting for black bass and for any reason do not care to take up that method, a very good substitute and a very efficient angling method may be found in strip-casting. It may be said with truth, also, that at times strip-casting is more efficient than casting from the reel, whether or not you have mastered the use of the short bait-casting rod and the quadruple casting reel. Variety, too, is the spice of angling, and often a change to the fly-rod—which is used for strip-casting—is quite welcome after continued use of the orthodox short casting rod.

Strip-casting for bass is adapted to both river and lake fishing, and either natural or artificial baits may be used. Since the advent of the numerous and generally very successful artificial baits as the result of the popularity of bait-casting, these are most used. The chances are that in order to take up strip-casting you will have to buy very little extra tackle—that is, if you are a fly-caster.

The fly-rod is used for strip-casting because, to obtain the best results, the reel-seat must be below the hand-grasp. **The Rod.** The rod should not be less than ten feet in length—for strip-casting purely, a ten-and-a-half-foot rod is none too long, but you will probably wish to use a rod which may also be utilized for fly-casting. As the cast is made by shooting the line through the guides of the rod, these should be of a style which will allow free-running of the line.

A fly-rod to be specially used for strip-casting would be best rigged in the matter of guides by using fairly large caliber German silver trumpet guides with agate hand and tip guides. If your fly-rod is fitted with "snake" guides, these will answer the purpose. The addition of the agate guides is very desirable in either case. A bass fly-rod weighing from seven to eight ounces is best adapted to strip-casting, but any trout fly-rod having sufficient backbone may be used.

The Reel. The reel may be either a single-action or a double-multiplier; the quadruple reel may also be used, but for certain reasons, such as lack of balance on the fly-rod and greater liability of line fouling, is not as well adapted to strip-casting as the reels mentioned. As a matter of fact the reel is not necessarily used to any extent in strip-casting except to hold the line. The single-action reel, all things considered, is the best.

The Line. There is considerable leeway in the matter of the sort of line to use. Strip-casting bears a closer analogy to bait-casting than to fly-casting in that the line is caused to shoot out through the guides by the swing of the rod and principally by the weight of the bait in use. It differs from fly-casting in that the weight of the bait, rather than of the line and the swing of the rod, is the chief factor in getting out the line. It naturally follows that a line having weight is not absolutely necessary as for fly-casting.

On the whole the best line to use is a rather small caliber enameled fly-casting line, say size G or F. This will render freely and smoothly through the rod guides and is much more durable and less liable to foul by wrapping around the rod than an unwaterproofed bait-casting line. For average bass fishing twenty-five yards of good quality size F enameled line used on a one-hundred-yard single-action reel will best answer the reel and line requirements for strip-casting.

The method of casting is very simple and yet, to acquire expertness and the very best results, no little practice and experience are required. Before going on

FINE AND FAR-OFF FISHING

to speak of the baits to use and the general course of action of the strip-caster when on the bass grounds it would, perhaps, be best to settle the question of how to use rod, reel, and line in strip-casting. This method is almost exclusively employed when fishing from a boat or canoe —seldom while wading, or from the bank of a river or the lake shore.

How to Cast.

The reel and line should be rigged on the rod as for fly-casting; that is, the reel underneath with the handle to the right. A short gut leader may be used if desired or one of fine steel or copper if pickerel or pike are abundant where your bass fishing is done. Very heavy baits, either artificial or natural, should not be used, as the work will be too strenuous for the fly-rod unless it is a very heavy and stiff one.

Assemble rod, reel, and line and have about six or eight feet of line from the tip of the rod. Now strip from the reel several feet of line, allowing the coils to lie in the bottom of the boat. Always be careful to lay it down so that it will not tangle and foul during the cast. A new enameled line which shows a tendency to coil tightly should be well straightened by rubbing down with deer fat or some other line dressing before attempting to use it for strip-casting.

The knack lies largely in educating the left hand to manipulate the line correctly. As in the practice of many fly-casters, the left hand grasps the line between the reel and the first guide and is used to control the rendition and retrieve of the line during and after the cast. If it is your custom to handle the line thus when fly-casting, you will not have to learn it; otherwise, although a limited proficiency may be quickly acquired, it will pay you to practice this phase of strip-casting faithfully; its importance is equal to that of thumbing the reel in bait-casting. During the cast the outrunning line must be subject to exactly the proper control, must run out neither too fast or too slow, or the line will foul at the first rod guide.

Having stripped the line from the reel, and controlling it as above indicated with the left hand, presuming that you are casting from right to left, carry the rod to your right and slightly to the rear, pointing a little downward toward the water, and then swing it smartly to the left across the body and slightly upward. When, during the swing of the rod, the rod tip points in the direction you wish to cast—as a matter of fact, just a little before that point—release the hold of the left hand on the line sufficiently to allow it to run out through the fingers. Do not release it entirely, as this will feed the line to the first rod guide faster than it will run through and a tangle will result. The cast is quite similar to the side cast in bait-casting from the reel.

The cast being completed, that is, the bait having reached the water at the desired point, the line is retrieved by stripping it in through the guides with the left hand, taking pains to lay the coils down evenly on the bottom of the boat as in the preliminary stripping from the reel. The line should be stripped in at a moderate rate of speed, rather faster with artificial lures than with natural, in order to impart lifelike

FINE AND FAR-OFF FISHING

motion to the bait, and care should be taken to have the line and rod always under control, so that immediate advantage may be taken of a strike.

The importance of a taut line should not be overlooked. After hooking a bass the fish is, of course, played "by hand" rather than from the reel, unless an extra long run takes out all the free line. This should not be considered a disadvantage, for, as a matter of fact, the very best and safest way to play a fish is by this method; that is, by controlling the giving and taking of line with the left hand independently of the reel.

Keep a Taut Line.

Light artificial baits are the best to use, such lures as small trolling spoons, fly-spinners, bucktail spoons, etc.; light-weight floating baits and pork rinds on small white enameled spoons are also very successful. Fly-spoons made in tandem style and used in connection with bass flies of well-known patterns, scarlet ibis, Parmachene belle, Montreal, coachman, Henshall, silver doctor, and others, are very pleasant baits to use and, moreover, quite acceptable to the bass; with these should go a small dipsey sinker. Fly-spoons of this sort are made in a great variety of styles and in several degrees of desirability; those with piano wire shanks and without swivels are the best.

The Baits to Use.

The most successful methods for the strip-caster to adopt when on the bass grounds are very similar to those used in bait-casting. Casting from a canoe or boat, the angler should work around the lake shore, casting in toward the rushes and

Methods.

lily pads and along the margin of the aquatic vegetation of the lake, and also over and along rocky or sandy bars, about spring-holes, at the inlet or outlet of the lake, and other similar places where the black bass "uses."

Necessary items in the outfit not mentioned above are a small tackle box and a landing net. The latter will save many large bass which would otherwise be lost by bungling attempts to get them into the boat—a six-ounce fly-rod is a mighty poor tool with which to "derrick" a four-pound bass.

Other Tackle.

A modification of strip-casting—or possibly fly-casting, as it is difficult to determine which method is most closely approximated—exists in the use of small, light fly-spoons in connection with single-hook bass flies (these fly-spoons are practically the same as those mentioned for use in strip-casting, but the smallest sizes should be used) on ordinary fly-casting tackle.

A Variation of Strip-casting.

In running water fly-casting for black bass is on a par, both as a sport and as regards its practicality, with fly-fishing for brook trout. Both the small- and large-mouth bass rise freely to the artificial fly when it is properly presented and under the right conditions, the large-mouth having the reputation of being generally the most willing to inspect the feathers. But the right conditions for bass fly-fishing unfortunately do not prevail in many parts of the country, running water of the proper depth for fly-casting and wading wherein bass, either large- or small-mouthed, exist in sufficient

FINE AND FAR-OFF FISHING 143

numbers to warrant good sport with the fly-rod is very difficult to find except in certain favored localities.

Usually the bass streams are deep and sluggish, necessitating the boat and the casting rod, or else, if the streams are rapid and shallow, the brook trout is the principal game fish found therein. Fly-fishing for bass in lakes also—well authenticated exceptions duly noted and filed for future and practical reference—is notoriously unremunerative.

However, by using the customary outfit for fly-casting, casting in very much the same way and using a small, feather-weight fly-spoon, the angler can have fairly good sport with the fly-rod and the black bass under any normal angling conditions. You must, however, be a pretty good fly-caster—know how to use your left hand as well as your right in casting the fly or fly-spinner and how to "shoot" your line at the finish of the forward cast—and you must also use a fly-spoon that is suited to the business in hand.

There is one manufacturer who makes a specialty of this sort of tackle, and, as is often the case, the product of this specialist is measurably in advance of the "just as good" offered by other makers of tackle in general. Since there is little or no trade competition in regard to these fly-spoons and the author therefore is not liable to be accused of odious comparison or entire lack of intelligence about fishing tackle, it might be well to say for the accurate information of the reader that the fly-spinners mentioned are known as the Hildebrandts.

It is necessary that the spoon blades be very light and thin; that heavy swivels, or for that matter any swivels at all, be avoided; and that the bass flies used with the spinners be well tied and true to pattern and dressed on the best grade of hooks. Any fly-spoon which answers the above requirements will do, others will not.

The fly-spoons made in tandem style, that is, with two small spoon blades leading the fly, may be especially recommended both for strip-casting proper and also for use on the fly-rod for casting as with the fly. As above suggested only the lightest and smallest spinners should be used for casting as in fly-fishing. When ready for the back cast, in this last style of casting, do not snap the spinner out of the water, but lift it out easily. The former method is apt to result disastrously in several ways. Single-hook bucktail spinners and also a similar fly-spinner known as the fox squirrel tail are very successful lures for strip-casting and small spoon casting with the fly-rod.

Any of the lighter weight surface baits such as are used in bait-casting are also good for strip-casting. It would appear that under certain conditions the black bass favors a floating bait; quite often they will rise to the surface and strike a floating lure when under-water fishing is barren of results. The floating baits are also the most practical and saving of tackle, fish, and temper when fishing very weedy lakes, casting among the lily pads and rushes, and in all places where under-water fishing is liable to result in fouling the tackle either in casting or after a bass is hooked. As a general rule, a bass which strikes a floating bait will fight close to the surface, seldom going down to any considerable depth, and the wise angler, either bait- or strip-caster, fishing where the bottom is badly obstructed will do well to remember this.

CHAPTER VIII

PROSPECTING WITH A CASTING ROD

On the Trail of the Black Bass

IT is a fact well known to students of human nature and angling, that a fisherman will often turn his back on good fishing near at hand for the sake of trying his luck on little, inconsequential ponds and rivers which no one ever heard of particularly but are darkly rumored to "swarm" with huge bass. Sometimes you do, indeed, catch a few bass; oftener you do not. Always you put in many hours of hard work tramping the woods, swinging a paddle or pulling the oars, and at the end of the trip invariably "Never Again" is your slogan.

Some little time thereafter, running over in your mind the various events of your latest prospecting fiasco, you realize that, after all, you have had a mighty good time; that it is not all of bass fishing to kill bass; and that on these little prospecting tours you experience to the fullest extent all of the things which make fishing really worth while—although you do not catch even one small bass.

The call of strange waters, little ponds "way off" in the woods, the upper reaches of rivers as yet unexploited by anglers, is practically irresistible. For a time, when camping out, the fishing is within easy reach from the camp. Then, no matter how fine may be the sport at the home-camp, a side trip on the chance of connecting with an imaginary record fish, or finding some purely hypothetical lake is always in order. The rightly constructed angler is an indefatigable explorer, although at least half the time and from the strictly practical point of view the object of his explorations is somewhat vague. It is manifestly foolish to leave first-class fishing for the merely supposititious sport afforded by some little known and possibly non-existent lake or river, but we all do it.

Just why a man will tear his way through the woods for days in order to reach a place where "the hand of man has never set foot," which, after all, is quite like any other place, is difficult to comprehend. And the mental status of the angler who pulls, pushes, and paddles a canoe and half a ton of excess baggage and fishing tackle up a river for the express purpose of wetting his line "farther up" than anyone else has ever been crazy enough to fish is, to say the least, unstable if not dangerous. Of course the reason is usually the supposititious larger fish and better fish in the presumably unfished waters. But the world is already pretty small and annually growing smaller, and every angler knows, or has reason to know that at the present stage of the game all the best fishing waters are neither lost, strayed, or stolen; their locations are definitely known and duly recorded in the railroad guide-books. This is from the common-sense point of view—which, of course, should be entirely disregarded as it has no bearing on the matter.

Just so long, however, as the old saw that it is not all of fishing to catch fish holds true, anglers will continue to chase the will o' the wisp of better fishing, or bigger fish, "farther up" or "farther in," anywhere, in fact, except where you are, always provided the place is sufficiently inaccessible. Inaccessibility of location makes a sporting proposition of any little old mud-bottomed pond that has nothing in it but bull-frogs, bull-heads, and possibly three or four slab-sided pickerel. Any duly accredited angler will risk his neck to fish such a place as this; and when, naturally, the trip turns out a brilliant failure, although he may protest strenuously against his "luck," way down in his heart he knows that he has got exactly what he went for —whatever that may be—and that, really, he is quite ready to do it all over again.

Fishing New Waters

Prospecting for black bass has, however, its practical side. To fish new waters successfully one should be pretty well acquainted with the habits of the bass in order to judge rightly as to their probable haunts and habits under the local conditions; and although certain phases of this subject have been discussed elsewhere, a review of the matters of this sort most pertinent from the present view-point, together with other facts knowledge of which will help the angler when prospecting new waters, will serve to emphasize their importance. Whenever possible it is well to call in the aid of some of the local talent, professional or otherwise, with a view to locating the game without loss of time. The black bass is a peculiar and undependable animal; even in ponds closely adjacent the habits and, to a slight extent, the color and formation of the bass respectively therein will differ. Particularly is there liable to be a difference in the kind of bait most favored. In one pond nothing but the natural baits, minnows, frogs, etc., will produce results; in another natural baits are of no use whatever while the various artificials—or, more frequently, one particular artificial—are at a premium.

Quite naturally the habits of the bass in any given lake are to a great extent dependent upon the character of the lake itself; that is, if bass habits are dependent upon anything but the own sweet will of Mr. Bass in person, to which latter theory the writer is sometimes strongly inclined. Thus in shallow, weedy lakes the bass will be found feeding at quite different times from those in deep, clear water ponds with rocky bottoms; and, of course, as regards waters having these characteristics, it is probable that in the shallower, weedy water you will find the large-mouthed bass, and in the deeper and rocky bottomed lake the small-mouth.

Also, from season to season, in the same lake, you are likely to find the old feeding grounds deserted and catch pretty nearly all your bass in new places, these new places being productive all through the season, while other spots, to all appearances quite as good, will yield nothing. All through the season, every day, you will take a bass or two off a certain patch of weeds or rushes, another at the point of an old tree fallen in the water, and in a number of other places which become well known to you. Eventually you "go the rounds" visiting these spots in rotation and seldom fishing the rest of the lake. But, in all probability, the next season you will have to start out prospecting again, to learn anew where the bass are living.

In view of these things it should be manifest that the angler when visiting new waters in search of bass is playing against heavy odds, particularly if his time is limited and the lake is a large one. Some time ago the writer and a friend—to say nothing of two excessively heavy pack baskets, two phenomenally weighty rifles, and two ridiculously ponderous oars—packed through the woods to a lake "swarming with large, gamey black bass." Arriving at the lake a little after noon we found the boat we had expected to use swamped in six feet of water and impossible to raise—the moral is obvious. So we prospected for a craft and found one, a fine little boat that leaked not a drop and floated like a duck and, wonder of wonders, was not locked. Later we learned that this was the only other boat on the lake. This craft we promptly requisitioned—and the morality of this is not so obvious.

While eating our lunch we visually prospected the lake, looking for the best fishing water; apparently it was all about equally good and very good. All around the lake shore were fine patches of weeds, lily pads, and rushes; here and there large boulders showed above the surface, indicating fine rocky bars; and many large pine trees had tipped over into the water affording ideal bass shelters. We knew that our time was limited and that much depended upon how and where we decided to fish. However, it all looked so favorable that we decided that if we fished around the south shore we would have all the bass we could carry on the long tramp home.

So, until dewy eve, we fished around the south shore —without even a strike. A few days thereafter we learned that on the next day two anglers fished the north shore, using bait-casting tackle quite similar to our own, and had the finest kind of luck. This shows the seamy side of bass prospecting.

If it is impracticable to summon the aid of a local angler or guide and time is no object, as when, for instance, you are going into camp on the lake, it is a very good plan to do your first fishing by prospecting with a trolling line. Trolling from the rod is always an effective method for taking bass and in this way, working slowly around the shores on the lookout for bars and other bass habitats, you soon learn the lay of the water. The places where you have a strike or catch a bass should be carefully noted by reference to some landmark on the lake shore. Then when you get out the casting tackle and are ready for the real business of the trip, you will know pretty nearly where to fish.

The most propitious places for bass vary considerably with the time of year and even with the time of day. Thus the wise prospector early in the season will look for the fish well in-shore among the weeds and rushes

PROSPECTING

and on the edges of rocky or sandy bars; in streams on the riffles and generally in the more shallow water. Fishing off bars, or on them, is almost always successful and the angler should take pains to spot every bar in the stream or lake.

As the season progresses and the bass seeking cooler waters move out into the deeper portions of the lake the angler must follow them. Casting over the bars and shallows at this time is only successful very early and late in the day when the bass are feeding in-shore. The dissimilarity of taste in the matter of natural and artificial baits shown by bass in even closely adjacent lakes, alluded to above, should be borne in mind by the angler fishing new waters.

The present tendency of bass fishermen, especially bait-casters, is strongly toward the almost exclusive use of artificial baits; from the standpoint of the practical angler, who uses bait natural or artificial as the circumstances seem to warrant, the exclusive use of spoons, artificial minnows, and surface baits, to the absolute exclusion of natural bait in any form, is not desirable. When fair success may be had with the artificial baits—even although at the same time heavier results could be had with natural bait—the use of the artificials is cleaner, simpler, and preferable. But fanatical adherence to the artificial baits, for any reason whatever, when the natural is evidently and exclusively preferred by the bass is difficult to justify.

The prospector for bass, then, should not bring in an adverse decision in regard to any certain pond or lake until a variety of baits have been tried and the bass found wanting, and even then it is quite possible that they wanted something else. The angler who favors the small-mouth bass, discrediting the merit of the large-mouth, should prospect only in certain places, while the angler who is satisfied with any sort of bass has a much larger field to cover.

It is not merely a bookish theory that the small-mouth in streams favors swiftly running water—much the same localities as are sought by the brook trout—while the large-mouth seeks quiet, weedy places. This has been proved to the writer many times and some times very strikingly. On the Housatonic in Connecticut, as an instance, where the dam of an electric power plant affords swift-water fishing below and still-water above, you will take exclusively small-mouth bass below the dam and large-mouths above it.

In lakes also the habitats of the two black basses are almost equally well defined, the small-mouths being found about the spring-holes, on rocky bars, and possibly at the inlet or outlet of the lake if there is an appreciable current at these places, or where, as at the mouth of a mountain brook, the water is of a lower temperature. Often the two basses co-exist in the same lake when the large-mouth is usually found in quiet, weedy bays, among lily pads and rushes, and where the bottom is soft.

As a method of quickly trying out new waters bait-casting is quite equal to trolling provided the caster does not spend too long a time in whipping out any one spot. As a matter of fact repeated casting over a restricted piece of water is seldom of use anyway; almost invariably if there is a bass in the immediate vicinity of the cast and he is in a rising mood, he will strike at the first or second cast; if he does not, subsequent casts in the same place will seldom persuade him. With one man at the oars or paddle and another to handle the casting rod, working around the lake shore slowly and without stopping to whip out any one place to a finish, it is possible to prospect new fishing grounds very quickly and effectively.

When casting from a boat or canoe a great deal depends upon the man at the oars or paddle. It is an open question who deserves the most credit for the successful landing of a big, hard-fighting game fish, the man behind the rod or the one who, by his skilful handling of the fishing craft, aids the rod at every stage of the game. The canoemen of the North aid the angler in his pursuit of salmon and square-tails. In the North and West the man behind the paddle or the oars is more than a small factor in the landing of mascalonge. Wherever there are bass, there, too, are the fin- and weather-wise boatmen, upon whose knowledge of feeding grounds and boat handling the sportsman tourist must largely depend.

At present the rowboat is in most general use for fishing purposes, but the canvas-covered canoe is constantly gaining in popularity, especially for stream fishing. There is also a general tendency in most all localities toward better boats. Some years ago it was the exception to find, save among privately owned boats, anything much better than a "pung," a blunt-nosed, leaky monstrosity with a chronic objection to direct progress either forward or backward. The introduction of the inexpensive, well built, and very serviceable steel boats has bettered the situation a great deal. For any fishing that is worth while, it is impossible to get a boat that is too good; that is, as regards lines and ease of handling.

CHAPTER IX

CASTS AT RANDOM WITH UNEXPECTED RISES

The Wideawake Angler

WHEN fishing a trout stream the man who keeps his mind on the business in hand is far more successful than the "contemplative" angler. Contemplation—we know that this, in view of the very familiar traditions of the gentle art, is almost sacrilegious—and real fly-fishing are strictly incompatible. Fishing in books, however, that is, in some books, and fishing in rivers and lakes are two quite different propositions. For successful fly-fishing the angler must be "right on his muscle" every minute. If he allows his attention to wander to the proverbial "beauties of nature" or indulges in "day dreams" in accordance with the tenets of the less practical literature of angling, a light creel is the logical result. The average sportsman, although not insensitive to the natural beauties of the stream, quite naturally prefers to make a good catch—not necessarily an excessive one.

Striking a trout that has risen to the fly is a matter

of quick eye, steady nerve, and constant watchfulness. Every fly-caster can recall days when, although the trout were rising freely, his catch was very light. It was not because the trout were rising short. It was merely because he was a bit off in his striking, a little too quick or too slow. He was not "on his nerve." In target shooting with the rifle the same conditions prevail. There are days when the expert marksman is unable to let-off at the right time. To repay one for such unhallowed occasions there are days when every rise is fastened with certainty.

When the cast of flies is on the water they must be closely watched in order to take immediate advantage of a rise, but when the angler is not engaged in actual casting he should watch for a rising trout or likely looking places for a cast. A fly cast over a trout that has just risen is pretty sure to bring results. Although you may have fished a certain stream many times, you are almost certain to find new places that are promising—if you look for them. Every year a trout stream changes, in accordance with the force of the spring freshets. On your first day out you may find old-time favorite pools filled in and practically ruined and you will find that here and there new pools have formed. Rapids have been shallowed to riffles and riffles deepened to rapids. Overhanging trees have finally toppled over into the stream. New lurking places for trout have been hollowed out beneath the banks. Every year you must learn the stream over again.

In almost every trout stream there are certain reaches which are practically barren of trout. The careful angler, however, during the first days of the season, will try out such places very thoroughly, for it is quite possible that the annual change in stream conditions may result in trout being found there. I remember very well such an occurrence. A trout stream that I have fished a great many times was always troutless in its lower waters, despite the fact that here the stream, as far as one could judge, was exactly suited to the fish. There were several short rapids leading into fine pools, many large, submerged boulders just right for trout to hide around and beneath, and the banks were thickly grown to pines. Yet for several seasons I fished this water from time to time without even a rise. The trout were not there. But the following season the first day over this same water put a dozen good trout in the basket, and to date the fishing there is fairly reliable. Something had occurred to bring in the trout; just what, it would be difficult to determine.

The wideawake angler, admitting for the purpose of contrast that the contemplative angler exists outside the pages of angling literature, a matter of some doubt, may not become an authority on the beauties of Nature in the abstract, but he learns a good bit about certain special phases of nature—fish, for instance. Some one has said that the best time to observe nature is when the fish aren't biting. This is undoubtedly true, but it is also an admission of inability to make the fish bite. That this is a pretty difficult thing, at times impossible, may be true, but, nevertheless, your hardworking, wideawake angler works hardest and is most wideawake when it is a case of making the trout rise or an empty creel. And herein is one of the most interesting phases of fishing. A good trout taken under difficulties, teased to the fly when most disdainful of it, is worth a dozen fool fish crazy for the fly to such an extent that one has only to offer the cast to have it accepted. Only the enthusiast, however, the true-blue, strenuous fly-caster, will long continue to hammer away at water to all intents and purposes trout-void.

A constitutional inability to quit, when every trout added to the score must be a trout earned by the hardest kind of work and the exercise of infinite patience and skill, is the hall-mark of the genuine fly-fisherman. To such a man continued ill success serves merely as an incentive to further effort. He seeks to discover just what are the conditions which are causing the trout to stay down. Arriving at some conclusion regarding this, he endeavors to meet the situation in the selection, arrangement, or use of his tackle. If the results show that his theory is wrong it is simply a case of trying another method. And a good many times he eventually hits upon the proper thing and then—.

On the other hand we all know the "quitter." He is anxious to be known among men as an "ardent angler," an "enthusiast." He talks fish and fishing to infinity and upon microscopic provocation. But on the stream a little hard luck quickly shows his class. His conversation waxes loud and rather more than impolitely emphatic. He talks about smashing the rod—"might just as well fish in a frog pond"—and thrashes about in the stream like a pointer dog in a mud-wallow. Finally he quits entirely—whereupon there is much joy among his companions. It is quite true that there are times and places when and where no amount of careful work will bring even slightly adequate returns and continued effort is futile. It is also true that the man who keeps his powder dry and his line wet generally has something to show for his pains.

Game Fish in Winter

The advantage to the hunter and angler of a good working knowledge of the habits and haunts of game and game fishes is generally conceded. The man who knows the life histories of the deer and grouse, the brook trout and the black bass, has little need of a guide, save in so far as a geographical knowledge of the country to be fished or hunted may be necessary, to show him where to look for trout or where not to look for grouse.

Given two hunters or anglers equally well outfitted in the matter of guns and tackle and equally good shots and casters, and the one who has taken pains in his tramps afield and along the streams to note carefully such habits of the quarry as may have a bearing on his sport will always make the better showing. There are, of course, artificially planted and preserved coverts and streams where the abundance and innocence of the game will make up for lack of skill with gun, rifle, or fly-rod; in such cases knowledge of how and where to look for game and fish is not an imperative factor for success.

Where game and game fish exist in this superabundance, getting them is purely a matter of being a good shot or casting a straight line; even the poor shot and the awkward rod handler may obtain enough birds or trout to salve the wounds to his pride caused by repeated misses with the gun or the usual misfortunes of the novice or the confirmed bungler with the fly-rod.

There is a certain fish and game preserve controlled by a number of amiable but quite unathletic gentlemen "from the City." Each year, just before the opening of the trout season, the superintendent of this preserve dumps into the stream which runs through it several hundred liver-fed, two-pound trout. A few days thereafter the amiable but quite unathletic gentlemen "from the City" come up and "catch 'em"—on worms. That is one sort of sport.

On the other hand, there is another trout stream not far distant, a hard-fished public stream, from which I am willing to wager that the not too strenuous gentlemen aforesaid could not take a half-dozen trout in a day's fishing—with worms or in any other way. Yet a friend of mine can usually show you fifteen or twenty good trout taken from this stream on flies almost any day. That is another sort of sport.

This is not saying that the amiable metropolitans are entirely lacking in the right spirit; the mere fact that they show a certain appreciation of what we mean when we say "trout fishing" is evidence of existence of the right idea. It is merely saying that sport of the right sort is a matter of skill plus experience and observation.

But knowledge of the open season habits of fish and game, while all that the sportsman absolutely must know, may well be supplemented with some familiarity with the life of game when the season is closed. The appeal of the wilderness and woodland in winter has been repeatedly described and may here be taken for granted; also, that the exercise of a long tramp along country roads, ice-bound streams, and through white forest lands is no bad thing should go without saying.

Winter observation of the habits of fish is a pretty difficult matter; as, indeed, is actual observation of stream life at any time. The things we know about trout and bass and other game fishes have been in great part gathered from observation of specimens in confinement in hatcheries and aquariums. By this is meant knowledge of the life of fishes apart from certain phases well known to any experienced angler. The trout stream in winter, banked with snow and, save in the rifts where the current is very broken and rapid, sealed with ice, offers little hint as to the life of its inhabitants.

That the trout brook of January after a fall of snow and in the sunshine is nearly, if not quite, as good to look at as the trout brook of June, is small consolation to the man who wants to know about trout. And yet it would appear that the sportsman who follows down his favorite stream when that stream is nothing more than so much snow and ice learns something about trout; just what, it would be difficult to put into words, but the fact remains that the angler who has an all-the-year-round acquaintance with his stream has a certain advantage over the man whose stream experience is limited to the spring and summer months.

The brook trout of the winter time is a very different fish from the brook trout of June. He is inactive, sluggish, and a bottom feeder. He does not go into retirement to such an extent as does the bass, but, nevertheless, is far from active. The brook trout feed more or less, rather less than more, during the winter, and sometimes ice fishermen, trap-fishing for pickerel and perch on lakes inhabited by the speckled trout, catch them through the ice.

In the Berkshires there is a small lake known as Three Mile. Three Mile brook is the outlet of the little lake and has brook trout. Naturally there are trout in the lake. Some time ago some winter anglers fishing through the ice with the ordinary "types" or pickerel traps used for the purpose took fourteen brook trout averaging a pound. The story does not tell whether they put them back or not, but that they caught the trout I know to be a fact. I might add that one of the best known and most skilful fly-casters in Massachusetts has repeatedly fished Three Mile Pond for brook trout during the open season, with flies and everything else except dynamite, but without success— not a single trout. This is a fine situation to theorize about, if you are given to theories.

Opening day trout fishermen have the best luck bottom-fishing with bait, and they will tell you that the trout of April first or fifteenth, as the case may be, although they take bait very freely, are extremely sluggish when hooked and when landed are found generally to be in poor condition. It would seem, then, that the brook trout is a light feeder in winter rather from lack of opportunity than from inclination, for the conditions prevailing early in April are usually distinctly wintry.

I have taken brook trout on bait standing in snow up to my knees; also in the worst of a heavy snowstorm. Under the same conditions trout have been taken on flies. Brook trout in October or November are found at the headwaters of streams and up the small tributary brooks where they resort during the spawning season. After the spawning season and during the winter months there must be a general drifting back to the main stream, and in the main stream a movement downstream to the usually deeper waters below.

The brook trout migrations mentioned by the naturalists, that is, a general movement up-stream prior to the spawning season, followed by a retreat to lower waters thereafter, are, however, not to be taken too literally; it should not be understood that at any time either the upper or lower reaches of the stream are entirely trout deserted. As in the summer, trout may be found about the spring-holes, so also in winter they are found there. In the summer they seek the vicinity of the spring-holes because there the water is cooler, but in winter because, rather curiously, it is then the warmer. Spring water is slow to freeze. The usual winter habitat of the brook trout is in the deeper holes and long, deep reaches of still-water.

Formerly there was considerable controversy about the so-called hibernating of the black bass during the winter months, but it is now definitely known that, when the streams and lakes are frozen, the bass do, indeed, hibernate in much the same manner as certain fur-bearers. Hibernation, however, does not imply complete cessation of the forces of life but merely a dormant state which, under certain circumstances, may be temporarily interrupted. Thus the basses, both large- and small-mouthed, when the water reaches a low temperature, seek refuge in the interstices of rocks, in hollow, submerged logs, and places of like nature, sometimes even burrowing into the mud of the lake bottom, where they remain for long periods inactive and without feeding.

But if several days of unseasonably warm weather should come, melting the ice and raising the temperature of the water, the bass would again become active. Also it is fairly certain that individuals remain active all winter; that is, all the bass in any given lake are not inactive at any one time. Ice fishermen quite often during the winter report catching a single, sometimes two or three, black bass. On one occasion a friend of mine, fishing through the ice of a river cove, took eleven black bass, large-mouthed, the heaviest weighing two and a half pounds. This is the heaviest catch of black bass through the ice that has ever come to my notice. The winter bass seeks the deep waters of stream or lake, coming to the shallows when the water grows warm in the springtime.

The winter habits of pike, pickerel, and perch are much the same as in the warmer months, although they are not so frequently found in shallow water. These fishes feed all winter and are quite active at all times. Ice-fishing for pickerel and perch, although hardly in the same class with fly-fishing for trout, is good fun and widely practiced.

Killing Time in a Fishing Camp

If the camp is a permanent one you will often have time to kill and you cannot do better than to use some of it in putting the fishing industry on a business-like basis. As a general rule camping is seldom done merely for the pleasure of life under canvas; that is, the camp is most often subordinate to the pursuits of fishing or hunting or some other outdoor sport. You should not allow all your attention to be taken up with the commonplace details of tents, outfits, cookery, and the like. If the fishing is to be successful there are several things to be looked to in this regard.

One of the first necessities is a rod rack. Possibly you will go into camp with the idea that, when through with it, you will take the rod down. It is quite probable that for the first two or three days you will do this. After that it is extremely doubtful. Something like the following comes to pass. You come in from fishing and are immediately assailed with a more or less polite request to rustle firewood—at once. You lean the split-bamboo against a convenient pine tree and do your duty. Then other things demand your attention. The rod is out of sight and mind. All night it leans against the convenient pine tree and by the next morning has acquired a beautiful set and is a fit candidate for the rod hospital. Now if there had been a rod rack this would not have happened.

If your quarters are large enough have the rack inside; if not, then under the tent-fly close to the tent where the rods will be protected and easy to get at in case of heavy rain. All you need is some crotched sticks. Plant them closely enough together so that the rod will be supported equally throughout its entire length.

For the bait-casting rods a better and more convenient arrangement, since these rods are short enough to allow this, is a rack on which the rods can be suspended from the tip. Such a rack can easily be constructed in several different ways and it hardly seems necessary to go into the details. It should be placed inside the tent and will take up very little room. Never by any chance allow a split-bamboo rod, or, for that matter, any rod, to lie for any length of time on the ground. It can be ruined in one night by this sort of treatment. By all means take the rod down if you can remember to; otherwise, use the rod rack.

In packing for a near-home trip, if you are not going light, it is a good plan to stow some of the outfit in a box which can be made into a live-bait box; or make your bait box at home and then utilize it for packing. Be sure to have the cover stout enough to hold the weights you will use upon it.

If you have a line dryer you will probably use it sometimes. A couple of cleats nailed one above the other to a tree or the tent pole make a competent dryer of which the most striking characteristic is simplicity. If you attempt a more complicated arrangement the chances are it will never be completed, unless you are one of those not rare individuals who may be described as "camp tinkers."

If the natural conditions are favorable it is a good

plan to have a pen where the surplus fish may be kept alive—if there is a surplus—so that when, as sometimes happens, the fish are off their feed for some length of time, it will not be a case of straight bacon.

The angler who camps beside his fishing has many advantages over the one-day fisherman. Not only can he choose the best days and the best time of day for fishing but he has every facility for learning the peculiarities of the fish in that particular lake, their hours of feeding, where to look for them, their taste in the matter of flies and baits, the effect upon them of various local conditions, and similar matters. These are things the knowledge of which makes for success and the angler in camp should not fail to observe them.

Canoe vs. Waders

It must be admitted at the start that the majority of fly-fishermen, if the stream conditions are at all favorable, would choose the waders. For this choice there are many reasons, all good ones. The fly-caster who has acquired his angling education on northern trout streams is never quite at home when casting from boat or canoe; and to the minds of many anglers wading the stream is a necessary accompaniment of the day's fishing if the occasion is to be enjoyed to the utmost.

The man in the waders undoubtedly gets into closer communication with the stream and its surroundings than does the canoeman. From the first pool or riffle he follows the stream through its various windings, learning as he can in no other way its peculiarities. Every trout stream is unique. To fish it successfully it must be learned, and the man who wades, soon acquires a good working knowledge.

Given a stream which may be fished by either method, canoe or waders, the question arises as to which method is the more apt to be effective. Wading a trout stream is quite a science in itself. Some anglers, not the majority in America at least, favor fishing or wading upstream. The reasons for this preference are many and logical. It is claimed that as trout customarily lie heading up-stream the angler casting from below is less liable to be seen; that the flies when so cast as to float down to the fish from above act more naturally than when worked more or less against the current; and that wading up-stream removes the possibility of alarming the trout or, at least, causing them to be suspicious by any disturbance of the stream bed, the dislodgment of small sticks, or muddying the water, the current, of course, carrying the news to the trout when the angler is working down-stream.

The advantages of wading down-stream in the typically swift trout stream are, however, very apparent to most experienced fly-casters. In the first place it is far more natural and certainly much easier to wade with the current than against it. It is generally possible to cast a sufficiently long line to do away with the possibility of being seen by the fish, and it is a question whether the flies if skilfully fished from above are not quite as attractive as when worked from below. And as to the matter of disturbing the stream bed the man who wades slowly and carefully can reduce the disturbance to a negligible quantity.

The man who wades enjoys absolute freedom from restraint. The canoeman is bounded by the gunwales of his craft. However, in the silence with which the canoe makes its progress there is an advantage. If care is taken in the matter of anchorage no possible warning is given to the fish. Also, if the stream is a large one, good places may be easily fished from the canoe which might be beyond the ability of the most expert fly-caster to reach when wading. In the case of over-fished waters the use of a canoe, if the stream has ordinarily been fished by wading, might spell the difference between a light creel and a heavy one.

When fishing a stream of this sort it may be taken for granted that the most accessible spots have been fished to death, and the angler who is wise and ambitious will devote himself to the more difficult places. The chances are that such spots have been very little fished, and possibly, in the case of some of them, not at all. In many trout streams of good size there are reaches of deep, swift-running water too deep to wade and where the banks are so brushy as to prevent casting from them. Such places are avoided by the average angler, the man who wades, and the use of a canoe in such waters should yield very weighty results.

Landing Net and Gaff

The number of game fish annually lost between the water and the creel through the unskilful use or the absence of a landing net or gaff probably approaches closely to the amount of the entire catch. The final netting or gaffing of a fish sufficiently played and ready to be landed is more than a mere detail; it requires skill, presence of mind, and, above all, coolness. Every angler can remember times when the bungling use of the net resulted in the loss of the "big one." Also, the bungler, if the fisherman did his duty on these occasions, should have no difficulty in recalling the particular disaster in which he figured.

In stream fishing for brook trout, however, the angler is usually his own netter, and if through his haste or lack of skill in handling the net, the especially large one gets away, he has no one to blame but himself. Landing a trout in still-water is a matter of no great difficulty. The fish can be gradually played in to the angler, and when he is ready to be taken out the net should be immersed and the fish led over it. Sudden motions should be avoided and the fish neatly meshed without touching him with the rim of the net.

Sometimes the lightest touch of the net will revive a played-out fish and he is off again like a flash. In view of this it is advisable before using the net to have a fair amount of slack line off the reel which should be held between the fingers of the rod hand so that it can be released immediately. Thus prepared, a final rally of the fish is not apt to result in his escape. Unless the trout was originally hooked very hard after a more or less protracted siege of playing, the hook often "hangs by a thread" in which case if the trout is snubbed in the least the hook will tear away, and frequently if any slack is given it will drop out.

Landing a trout in fast-running water is another thing. Here, if the fish is a large one, the angler has his work cut out for him. The best plan is not to attempt to play the fish up to you but to hold him, as far as can safely be ventured, where he is hooked, and work down to him. If you try to drag him up-stream it brings him to the surface where he will roll over and over and thrash about until nine times out of ten he whips himself off the hook. Once down to the fish so that you do not have to handle him from above, but from the side or below, lead him gradually into a gentle side current. The fish should be up-stream from you when you are ready to use the net. The current will then bring him over the net instead of taking him away from it.

When fishing from a boat or canoe the net should have a handle at least four or five feet long. Almost invariably a bass that has been played in to the boat will take one more run when he sees it, and unless he is absolutely played to a finish he will always fight away from the boat. For fish that run large, such as the lake trout, a gaff should be used. Gaffing a fish should be gone about in the same way as when using the net. The gaff should be immersed and the fish led over it. A skilful gaffer will take a fish in out of the wet with one motion.

Although some anglers advise that even when there are two men in the boat, it is better for the man who is playing the fish to do his own netting, it would seem that it is preferable for the angler whose rod is not busy to handle the net. It is much easier to lead the fish within landing distance of the man who occupies the opposite end of the boat than to lead it in where you can net it yourself.

The Trolling and Casting Spoon

With the advent of the short bait-casting rod and the free-running reel has come an increase of interest in artificial lures. Bass fishermen of an experimental turn of mind are kept busy trying out each new bait as it makes its appearance, and the collections of these lures which some enthusiasts have made are indeed fearful and wonderful to behold. The non-angling person if shown one of these museums, without explanatory remarks, would be inclined to believe that it was the life work, complete to date, of an extremely ingenious maniac. With all this interest in the new and sometimes fantastic lures, not that some of them do not catch bass, the old and very reliable "spoon hook" has suffered a temporary eclipse. And yet, taking everything into consideration, the spoon is without doubt the best of all-round artificial bait ever invented. Upon it, when skilfully and seasonably used, every important game fish of fresh waters may be taken. Its attractive motion when in action is hardly equalled by any of the later inventions, and as a casting bait it may always be relied upon.

The original spoon was merely a spoon-shaped blade with a hole at one end for attaching the line and at the other end a single hook was fixed. It caught fish. Since then the tackle dealers have put on the market manifold variations of the original, some of them sufficiently ingenious, but none of them in any way more consistently successful than the standard trolling and casting spoon as it is now furnished. The different forms of these variations are entirely too many to be considered. One variation, however, it might be well to mention. Spoons are furnished in several different materials, the principal ones being nickel, brass, copper, silver, and gold. As between these forms when in use the brass, copper, or gold spoons are less flashy in effect. Many anglers affirm, with reason, that in accordance with the well-known rule as to the use of artificial flies, the less noticeable spoons are more successful in very clear, bright weather.

As to whether the tuft of feathers with which the trebles of most spoons are furnished is advantageous, there is a decided difference of opinion. Their original excuse was probably merely as a concealment for the hooks. As far as this is concerned they are useless. Concealment is unnecessary. The question is rather as to whether the addition of the feathers renders the spoon more attractive. In this regard expert opinion seems to favor the feathers for bass, while as regards pickerel and pike it is a matter of indifference. As the feathers are usually tied there is a generous sprinkling of red; and as the black bass is known to have a strong predilection for this color it would seem that, since the use of the feathers is hardly a definite disadvantage, the wise angler should at least hesitate before following the advice of those who advocate the use of the bare treble or single hook in connection with the spoon.

In reading the authorities it is the duty of the layman to believe implicitly all that he reads and, as far as possible, to go and do likewise—otherwise of what use are authorities? Sometimes, however, this is a matter of no little difficulty, for these gentlemen of great experience along similar lines quite frequently arrive at exactly contrary conclusions.

Here is an example. William C. Harris held the opinion that the use of a spoon in connection with a minnow rendered the minnow much more effective. Dr. James A. Henshall has stated that, in his opinion, this use of a spoon is not only of no advantage but that "moreover, it savors of pot-fishing." And there you are. In view of this, it would seem that others are entitled to a very firm opinion one way or the other. The consensus of opinion is probably that a small spoon so rigged as to lead the minnow is an advantage. The flash of the revolving metal, easily seen at a greater distance than the natural sheen of the minnow, attracts the fish from a wider area than would the minnow alone, with the result that they eventually strike the bait.

The Way of a Trout With a Fly

Of all forms of angling fly-fishing is the most intrinsically interesting and the most productive of varied and sometimes remarkable experiences. The stream fly-fisherman of many seasons is perforce learned in the ways of the brook trout. In fair weather and foul, at times successfully and at other times with ill success, he has cast his flies over many waters and been in at the death of many good fish. But, withal, the way of a trout with a fly is still to him much of a mystery. There are, in general, in every stream three characteristic localities wherein at some time the trout will rise to a fly; these are the riffles, rapids, and pools. In each of these places the rises, as a rule, will show certain fairly well sustained differences; that is, to take the conditional extremes, the trout of the quiet water will rise to the fly quite differently from his brother of the rapids.

Dependent upon the time, early, well along, or late in the season, trout are found on the riffles in lesser or greater numbers and at night large trout resort there when feeding. But as a rule the trout of the shallow riffles are not large. They strike very quickly, frequently miss, and fastening them is a matter of quick eye and good judgment, to say nothing of an educated wrist. In the pools the conditions are reversed. Here the fish are apt to be weighty and their method of rising and taking the fly is in dignified keeping with their size. The angler must adapt his course of action to the occasion. Also the question of what fly and how fished can usually be decided only by actual trial.

In regard to the construction of the artificial fly some fly-fishing theorists hold that coloration is of chief importance and others maintain that color should be subservient to form. The practical fly-fisherman is unwilling to subscribe entirely to either theory. Minute differences and gradations in coloration or form do not appeal to the practical man as being of sufficient importance to warrant the hair-splitting and ink-shedding in which their advocates indulge. And yet it must be admitted that almost every angler can cite from his own experience an occasion when some such slight variation of shade or shape proved the deciding factor in the day's success.

Every angler likes to fish a new, well-tied fly. There are times, however, and this is worth remembering, when the oldest, most frayed out nondescript in the fly-book will succeed despite the fact that the latest spring fashions in artificial bugs have failed dismally. Such a ragged veteran as this, with a torn wing and body partly unravelled and trailing, seems at times to have an almost hypnotic influence over reluctant fish. The grizzly king, a very good general fly bordering on the fancy, is usually tied with a red tail. As an instance of the occasional importance of small differentiations in the artificial fly it may be said that in some localities this fly is of almost no use unless the red tail is removed.

As a rule the fly-book of the experienced angler contains flies of comparatively few patterns in regard to color, while as regards variation of size the range is wide. Every fly-caster comes in time to depend upon a certain few flies which have served him well, and a plentiful supply of these favorites dressed on hooks of various sizes, is all that he asks. The coachman is the most generally useful trout fly and aside from it there is no other fly upon which two anglers are wont to agree. While it is true that a restricted fly list is wholly competent on waters which the angler has fished many times and knows like a book, it is also true that in strange waters the angler who plays his aforetime favorites to the exclusion of reputedly successful local patterns is inviting disappointment.

Fishing the fly, when all is said, is of far more importance than either the formation or coloration of the fly. The operation of casting may, to a certain extent or natural limit of proficiency, be learned by almost anyone. Fishing the fly is quite another matter and herein the angler shows his quality. To fish successfully with the fly the angler must have "fish sense."

THE END